FOUL DEEDS & SUSPICIOUS DEATHS IN & AROUND CARLISLE

FOUL DEEDS AND SUSPICIOUS DEATHS Series

Wharncliffe's *Foul Deeds and Suspicious Deaths* series explores, in detail, crimes of passion, brutal murders and foul misdemeanours from early modern times to the present day. Victorian street crime, mysterious deaths and modern murders tell tales where passion, jealousy and social deprivation brought unexpected violence to those involved. From unexplained death and suicide to murder and manslaughter, the books provide a fascinating insight into the lives of both victims and perpetrators as well as society as a whole.

Other titles in the series include:

Foul Deeds and Suspicious Deaths in Birmingham, Nick Billingham
ISBN: 1-903425-96-4. £10.99

Foul Deeds and Suspicious Deaths in Bolton, Glynis Cooper
ISBN: 1-903425-63-8. £9.99

Foul Deeds and Suspicious Deaths in Colchester, Patrick Denney
ISBN: 1-903425-80-8. £10.99

Foul Deeds and Suspicious Deaths in Coventry, David McGrory
ISBN: 1-903425-57-3. £9.99

Foul Deeds and Suspicious Deaths Around Derby, Kevin Turton
ISBN: 1-903425-76-X. £9.99

Foul Deeds and Suspicious Deaths in & around Durham, Maureen Anderson
ISBN: 1-903425-46-8. £9.99

Foul Deeds and Suspicious Deaths in Hampstead, Holburn & St Pancras, Mark Aston
ISBN: 1-903425-94-8. £10.99

Foul Deeds and Suspicious Deaths in Hull, David Goodman
ISBN: 1-903425-43-3. £9.99

Foul Deeds and Suspicious Deaths Around Leicester, Kevin Turton
ISBN: 1-903425-73-1. £10.99

Foul Deeds and Suspicious Deaths in London's East End, Geoffrey Howse
ISBN: 1-903425-71-9. £10.99

Foul Deeds and Suspicious Deaths in London's West End, Geoffrey Howse
ISBN: 1-845630-01-7. £10.99

Foul Deeds and Suspicious Deaths in Manchester, Martin Baggoley
ISBN: 1-903425-65-4. £9.99

Foul Deeds and Suspicious Deaths in Newcastle, Maureen Anderson
ISBN: 1-903425-34-4. £9.99

Foul Deeds and Suspicious Deaths Around Newport, Terry Underwood
ISBN: 1-903425-59-X. £9.99

Foul Deeds and Suspicious Deaths in and Around Scunthorpe, Stephen Wade
ISBN: 1-903425-88-3. £9.99

Foul Deeds and Suspicious Deaths in Stratford & S. Warwickshire, Nick Billingham
ISBN: 1-903425-99-9. £10.99

More Foul Deeds and Suspicious Deaths in Wakefield, Kate Taylor
ISBN: 1-903425-48-4. £9.99

Foul Deeds and Suspicious Deaths in York, Keith Henson
ISBN: 1-903425-33-6. £9.99

Foul Deeds and Suspicious Deaths on the Yorkshire Coast, Alan Whitworth
ISBN: 1-903425-01-8. £9.99

Please contact us via any of the methods below for more information or a catalogue.
WHARNCLIFFE BOOKS
47 Church Street – Barnsley – South Yorkshire S70 2AS
Tel: 01226 734555 – 734222; Fax: 01226 724438
E-mail: enquiries@pen-and-sword.co.uk
Website: www.wharncliffebooks.co.uk

Foul Deeds & Suspicious Deaths In & Around
CARLISLE

IAN ASHBRIDGE

Series Editor
Brian Elliott

Wharncliffe Books

First Published in Great Britain in 2006 by
Wharncliffe Local History
an imprint of
Pen and Sword Books Ltd.
47 Church Street
Barnsley
South Yorkshire
S70 2AS

Copyright © Ian Ashbridge 2006

ISBN: 1-845630-15-7

Typeset in 10/12pt Plantin by Concept, Huddersfield.

Printed and bound in England by
Biddles Ltd.

Pen & Sword Books Ltd incorporates the Imprints of
Pen & Sword Aviation, Pen & Sword Maritime,
Pen & Sword Military, Wharncliffe Local History,
Pen and Sword Select, Pen and Sword Military Classics
and Leo Cooper.

For a complete list of Pen & Sword titles please contact
PEN & SWORD BOOKS LIMITED
47 Church Street
Barnsley
South Yorkshire
S70 2BR
England
E-mail: enquiries@pen-and-sword.co.uk
Website: www.pen-and-sword.co.uk

Contents

Author's Note

There is one small point in the following work, which probably requires clarification. Though long known as Cumberland, the name of the county reverted back to its original name of Cumbria under the Local Government Act of 1974. However, the county is usually referred to in this instance as Cumberland, as it was invariably known during the entire period of foul deeds and suspicious deaths covered here.

Acknowledgements

n the writing of *Foul Deeds and Suspicious Deaths in and around Carlisle*, I owe a special debt of gratitude to Steve White and other members of staff at Carlisle Library, who have once again borne so patiently with my requests for articles, pictures and maps. Likewise I thank those at Carlisle Records Office, who placed similar material at my disposal and were invariably encouraging as always.

I would also like to pay tribute to those journalists whose assiduous coverage of the local crime scene over bygone years continued to fill numerous gaps in my knowledge, and to F Clive-Ross, for his enlightening article on the Croglin Vampire. Nor must I omit to mention the authors of those books which are listed along with my own earlier contribution at the rear of this work, several of which provided invaluable information on local history previously less well known to me, as well as other background information. A number of these books are available in the library of The Literary and Philosophical Society of Newcastle upon Tyne. I remain grateful to staff there too, who assisted me as necessary, as well as those at The National Archive, Kew.

I am indebted to my nephew, Andrew Richardson, who took many of the photographs utilized here, over and above those items, which Carlisle Library, Cumbrian Newspapers Ltd., and the Chief Constable of Cumbria allowed me to reproduce. I also have my friend, Adrienne Storey to thank once again. Without Adrienne's computer skills and unflagging loyalty and patience, I would have found this project all the more difficult to complete. Last but not least, I am exceedingly grateful to my commissioning editor from Wharncliffe Books, Rupert Harding, for all his advice and unswerving encouragement.

Introduction

The history of Carlisle and its surrounding countryside has been one of violent death, deprivation and ill fortune over the centuries. Indeed, it has been said that the history of the border city is the history of the whole of present day north Cumbria. For whoever took the city, strategically placed on three rivers and controlling the main route into Scotland, could dominate virtually the entire region. Add to this, the fact that Carlisle itself was long starved of industrial development, with a dearth of minerals and other natural wealth about it, and it is easier to appreciate that its people were particularly well attuned to hardship as well as danger, with the gibbet on Harraby Hill a constant reminder of what could happen were they to step too far out of line, even on their own midden.

By the end of the eighteenth century, compared with many other northern towns and cities caught up in the upheaval of the industrial revolution and all its accompanying misery, Carlisle and the area about it probably remained a trifle less inundated by the growing crime rate elsewhere in the country, its people simply wanting to get on and enjoy a standard of living which had already been more available in other parts of the UK. Yet there was growing crime there too. True, in Carlisle itself, there were to be less than a dozen murders listed during the entire nineteenth century. The total was higher beyond the city boundaries, but still low compared with many regions.

Nevertheless, there was an increase in crime of most kinds there, given the recent huge surge in population due to industrialization and improved transport facilities, all against a backdrop of fluctuating employment, low wages and abysmal working and living conditions now experienced by the majority everywhere. There was an increase in drinking and domestic violence. More turned to petty crime in the new machine-loving age, just to survive. Other deeds of a more insidious kind remained; many single parents for instance, driven to desperation, continued to dispose of their unwanted infants at birth. Charges of manslaughter still tended to replace those of murder on occasions. What murders there were tended to remain as heinous as any elsewhere. All this and more affords sufficient material for a fascinating study of the lengths many were still prepared to go to, given the multifarious pressures upon them before and since in and around Carlisle, despite the miseries and controls of the past.

Carlisle Court Houses and the new gaol in 1829. Author's Collection

We commence here with an account of the history of the old city and the area about it, before concentrating essentially on the nineteenth century when most of our stories occur. These are grouped randomly to afford variety. Not every foul deed or unsavoury death is touched upon but many are. We also go back again on occasion to previous centuries and into the twentieth century. All in all, five centuries are covered with full emphasis on the darker side of humankind, Carlisle and its surrounding region proving no different to many another in this respect, though naturally, there were some who remained much more degenerate than others, and those who never offended at all.

Background

Carlisle owes its origins to the Romans, who quickly recognized its site as providing a strategic defence against enemies further north. They built a fort of turf and wood where the cathedral now stands around AD 80. Leaving a garrison there, they continued on into Scotland on an abortive mission of conquest. Some decades later, the Emperor Hadrian decided to pull out of Scotland altogether and ordered construction of a great wall from the mouth of the Tyne to the Solway, to mark the frontiers of his empire. This has been known ever since as Hadrian's Wall. A considerable community sprang up within the environs of the original fort with a garrison of some 1,000 men catered for by the local natives. By this time the Romans were well established throughout the region. Their presence was not always accepted wholeheartedly. Around AD 200 there occurred a violent rising of Celtic tribesmen in the Lake District. This was put down ruthlessly as was any other dissent but by and large, the region remained peaceful and Carlisle began to take shape.

The Romans finally departed around AD 390. Little is known about Carlisle, or Luguvalium, as it had first been known, over the next few hundred years. But by the time of St Cuthbert, in AD 685, it was commonly known as Luel. Presently the Celtic word 'caer' meaning 'fort' was added, and the place became known as Caer-luel, which would eventually be abbreviated to Carlile or Carlisle.

In the meantime, the local tribes began fighting among themselves and became so divided that they were an easy prey for Danish invaders, who are said to have massacred the entire population of Carlisle and razed the place to the ground shortly before the beginning of the tenth century. The whole area became a wilderness for some time. It presently fell under the maw of the Scots, who ruled there until 1070. Following the brief rule of Dolfin, Earl of Northumberland, William Rufus took the re-emerging town in 1092 and built the castle, appreciating the strategic importance of the place as the Romans had done. It would be the onset of a fresh wave of hard and bloody times for the local people, continuing off and on for several centuries.

Though the Normans did establish order of sorts for a while in and around Carlisle, gave it a cathedral and continued to fortify the place itself, this order would not be lasting, given the proximity of Scotland and its uneasy natives. In 1135 they again seized Carlisle and were installed there until 1157, when Henry II drove them out. Disputing

Carlisle Cathedral, where Jacobite prisoners were incarcerated in 1745–46. Andrew Richardson

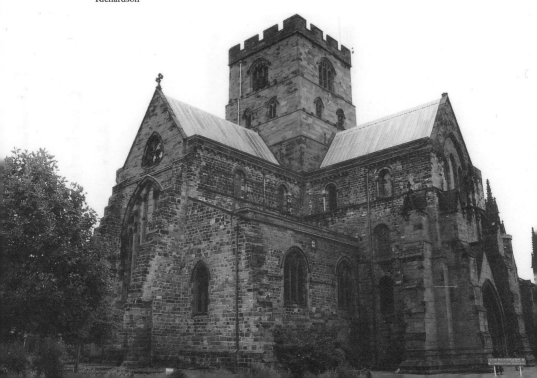

the English claim, they besieged Carlisle for several months in 1174 to no avail, but finally took the city again in 1216 for a few months before retreating back to Scotland. Thereafter there were some decades of uneasy peace but in 1292, the city was all but wiped out by fire.

During succeeding years, Edward I used Carlisle as his head-quarters, while following through on his pathological determination to impose English rule on Scotland, giving rise to hatred throughout the region. Thus the city once again found itself under siege in 1296. That same year, a Scottish spy attempted to burn down the castle, doing considerable damage. Edward I, who preferred towards the end of his life to reside at nearby Lanercost, died on Burgh Marsh in 1307. Following this, Robert Bruce attacked Carlisle and was only beaten off through the organizational skills of the Castle Governor, Sir Andrew de Harcla, later to be cruelly executed by his own side for alleged treason.

It was additionally unfortunate for Carlisle and the surrounding region that no definite border between England and Scotland had ever been established. The whole border area became known as the debatable lands. Though the time did eventually come when Scots and English were not perpetually at war, those inhabiting the undefined territories, Armstrongs, Grahams, Croziers, and other villains, were constantly on the move, stealing, burning, raping and pillaging, a law unto themselves, north of the city and elsewhere.

Meanwhile, Carlisle itself was going into a decline, a sink of poverty and disease, its population, though not lacking courage and stamina, nevertheless feeling increasingly dispirited by all the disorder and violence about them. They could never feel totally secure and few had bettered themselves, living as they continued to do in a part of the country well removed from any kind of vibrant commerce. To add to their misery, the Black Death carried off more of them in the middle of the fourteenth century. Neither were they yet to be ever totally free of the Scots, who besieged the city afresh in 1380, 1385, and again in 1387. Shortly after this there was another fire in the city, ravaging many of the wooden buildings.

In 1461, Carlisle was caught up in the Wars of the Roses and once again the Scots invaded. It was only thanks to the sadly maligned Duke of Gloucester, the future King Richard III, who governed the area from Penrith Castle for a number of years, that peace was eventually maintained again for some time.

Nonetheless, threats of invasion from Scotland and pillaging by the border clans remained. 1542 did see the Scots humiliatingly defeated near Longtown, following the failed Pilgrimage of Grace,

Penrith Castle, former headquarters of Richard III. Andrew Richardson

when seventy-five of the marchers were hanged at Carlisle, but it still behoved the locals to be wary.

Elizabeth I came to the throne in 1558. Parsimonious though she was, Elizabeth was another monarch who appreciated the strategic value of Carlisle. She allocated money to have many of the decaying defences repaired. The city again came to her attention when Mary Queen of Scots fled south in 1568 and arrived uninvited in the county. Elizabeth was well aware that her second cousin could pose a dangerous threat. Ostensibly she was not unsympathetic. Mary was given accommodation in Carlisle Castle and treated well. However, the Scottish queen soon realized she was a prisoner in all but name, watched constantly by insidious keepers. She would never be free again, leaving Carlisle some weeks later on a continuing journey south, which would ultimately end in her execution.

Like all the Tudors, Elizabeth was less positive in her handling of the Anglo-Scottish reivers, who continued to threaten the border region. It did prove possible to capture one of their notorious god-fathers, Kinmont Willie Armstrong, in 1596 and lodge him in Carlisle Castle. But his followers promptly sprang him during a storm, making something of a mockery of Elizabeth's earlier outlay on defence. This was particularly galling insofar as Carlisle's citizens were concerned. But worse was to follow. The plague returned in 1598, carrying

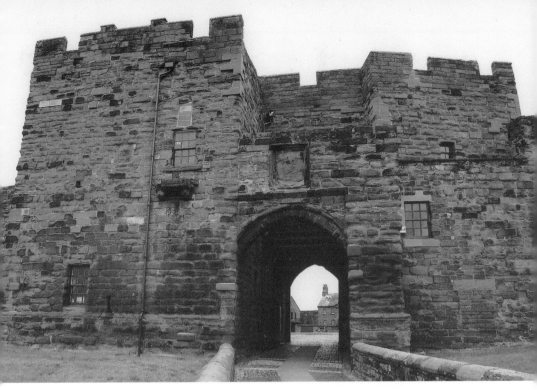

Entrance to Carlisle Castle, a place steeped in murky history. Andrew Richardson

off many of the city's inhabitants. And in 1599 their mayor was murdered by another of the border outlaws from the Graham clan, all against a background of persisting poverty. Any trade there was in the area still centred mainly around the city's weekly market, with its simple emphasis on exchange and barter.

Relief of a sort was to come following the death of Elizabeth in 1603 and the subsequent Union of the Crowns. The accession of James VI of Scotland as ruler of both kingdoms saw the first visit of a monarch to Carlisle for many years. As we have already seen, a number of the new king's predecessors had already recognized the value of Carlisle's strategic position, as well as the usefulness of smaller towns and villages about it, notably Penrith, Cockermouth and Lanercost, and there had been charters galore. But not all had visited the region personally. Therefore James was all the more lavishly entertained and prevailed upon to do something for the benefit of Carlisle itself. In the event, though happily taking a purse filled with gold and a valuable cup, presented by representatives of the needy citizens, he did nothing. On the other hand, his accession did spell the gradual demise of the reivers, given that there were no longer any debatable lands to sustain them. Within a few years they were no more, even while the borderlands were still infested by a variety of other felons.

This curtailment of the power of the Armstrongs and their satellites was sufficient of itself to endear the local population to the Stuart dynasty. Unfortunately however, James's successor, Charles I, was to bring misery of a totally different kind to the city. When the Civil War came, Carlisle remained under siege by Cromwell's forces for eight months and the citizens were reduced to eating dogs and rats. The city finally surrendered but was soon recaptured by the Royalists. But then Cromwell won it back again. Part of the recently restored cathedral was wantonly destroyed and there was further loss of life with fighting extending to the fringes of the Lake District.

Anyone taken prisoner then must have had a very hard time, more so if they were confined in Carlisle Castle dungeons, as many had been over the centuries. It remained not uncommon for prisoners there to be pinned upright against the wall by their necks in almost total darkness for indefinite periods. Conditions in the city gaol at the end of the west wall were almost as bad. George Fox the Quaker was locked up there for his preaching activities in 1653 and wrote of the filth and squalor amongst thieves and murderers, with one woman almost eaten to death by lice.

We do not know the precise extent of the offending in the city or its surrounding area during those years. It has to be borne in mind that the population of Carlisle itself remained comparatively low and was still no more than 2,000 by the time of the Act of Union with Scotland in 1707, having been decimated at intervals by war and plague. However, that there was some continuing offending there can be little doubt, with persisting reference to the gallows on Harraby Hill south of the city. They even merit colourful mention by Sir Walter Scott in his eighteenth century novel, *The Heart of Midlothian*. There is a particularly detailed account of the use of the *Harribee* gallows by George Mounsey following the 1745 occupation of the city by Prince Charlie's troops, when a number of Scottish prisoners were hung, drawn and quartered, but more of that later. Those hanged otherwise were probably highwaymen and common thieves in the main. Such is the impression given by occasional surviving records.

Towards the end of the eighteenth century, it became the norm to hang offenders on Carlisle Sands, close to the River Eden. Records have survived of several such executions, though precise information is brief. August 1788 saw two men turned off for burglary. In September 1791, another offender, Thompson, was executed for horse stealing. In September 1792, a trio were all hanged for similar offences. Seven years later there was an execution for forgery and the following year, 1800, when records begin properly, another forger, Alexander McGowan, the son of a shepherd, was turned off.

Towards the Nineteenth Century and Beyond

By and large, the beginning of the eighteenth century was at times probably little more devoid of violence and deviance than those before it in Carlisle and the area about it. Yet changes were afoot too, in a subtle kind of way. Though many did not realize it at the time, 1745 would be the last time Carlisle would find itself under siege. Indeed, Prince Charlie's abortive invasion from Scotland would indirectly lead to changes affecting the whole social structure of the area, to be fuelled by the looming industrial revolution, spearheaded by English and Scots alike, but bringing with it too at times, continuing deprivation, agitation and a fresh wave of crime.

Until the 1745 invasion, Carlisle and district had remained all but cut off from the remainder of the country as a whole, reached primarily by a mediocre road through Kendal and Penrith, with the old Roman road from Newcastle in a complete state of disrepair. No road to Carlisle could yet sustain very heavy transport, with continuing dependence on pack-horses. This was a prime reason why Prince Charles Edward was able to take the city so easily in 1745 from the north, English troops being so slow to arrive. Physically as well as economically, Carlisle had long remained starved of viable means of communication, or commercial opportunity either, surrounded by

smaller towns and villages with their own problems. Over and above this state of affairs as already noted, it had no mineral resources to hand and no established industries. Even some years after 1745, it was still deemed by one visitor to be a small under-populated place, neither impressive nor very prosperous it seems. That would now begin to change, with improved means of communication instigated by General Wade, to prevent any repeat of the 1745 debacle.

Perhaps ironically, the area's early ventures into commerce were indirectly linked to the slave trade. One man who quickly saw the potential inherent in the new military road to and from Newcastle, laid following Wade's recommendations, was Richard Ferguson (1716–1787), of

Charles Edward Stuart. Carlisle Library

Westlinton. Along with the Hodgsons, a moneyed family from Bascodyke, he began exporting coarse linen cloth woven from borderland flax. This was sent to West Africa. The ship involved was then filled with slaves and continued on to America, returning to Europe with raw cotton, spirits and tobacco.

Ferguson based himself at Carlisle. By the beginning of the nineteenth century he had also moved into cotton and textile printing. His sons carried on the business, being joined by Peter Dixon of Whitehaven, who married into the family. Dixon was responsible for the building of the huge mill in Shaddongate with its accompanying chimney, originally 305 feet high and still a great landmark. There was a massive increase in population given the weaving work now available locally. Many who flocked into the city, finally to be denuded of its crumbling walls, were Scots and Irish, who found partners among the indigenous natives, themselves a sturdy mixture of Celt, Angle and Saxon.

By 1800 the population of Carlisle stood at 10,000 and was still rising. In 1823 the canal to the Solway Firth was opened to great fanfare. The railways followed and the city became a principle rail centre and continued to expand. Eventually it had a huge biscuit factory, engineering works and breweries. But all was not quite as it seemed.

Since the majority of the city's workforce continued to rely on textiles for their livelihood, they long remained subjected to its fluctuations and fashion vagaries. This led to misery at times almost as bad as when the city had been subjected to siege and warfare. One interesting document published in those times is *The Struggles of a Hand-Loom Weaver*, the autobiography of William Farish, born in 1818, whose parents were both weavers in Carlisle. Farish tells of the

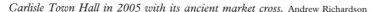

Carlisle Town Hall in 2005 with its ancient market cross. Andrew Richardson

appalling sufferings of those who followed the vagaries of the loom. A self-educated man, who later became a schoolteacher, he wrote:

It was no uncommon thing for our house to be without bread for weeks together; and I cannot remember to have ever seen, in my very early years, a joint of meat of any kind on my father's table; oatmeal porridge and potatoes, with an occasional taste of bacon being our principal food. Once, for six long and weary weeks at a spell, no bread entered the door; that extreme restraint being needed to enable my father to pay a few shillings of rent in arrears.

A persisting problem was the huge cost of haulage to and from Manchester and Liverpool where the principle textile markets were situated, affecting trade and creating constant instability. Revolutions and wars could also impinge. In 1812 and 1813, during the Napoleonic conflict, there were hunger riots in Carlisle and a local mill was attacked. In 1819, the city weavers voted to petition the Prince Regent to send them to America. By 1838, weaver's wages had been reduced by twenty per cent in the city. Matters came to a head with the onset of the American Civil War in 1861 and the subsequent abolition of slavery. Peter Dixon, who had been intermittently employing around 8,000 local workers, went bankrupt. Though trade soon revived in Lancashire and elsewhere, Carlisle was less fortunate. From then onwards, the cotton business locally was conducted at a lesser level. It never fully regained its former momentum.

Other firms and concerns in the city usually continued to function. It wasn't all doom and gloom. But wages were never high, hours were long, and accommodation often substandard, hence the upsurge in drinking, domestic violence and petty crime. And naturally there remained those who, for a variety of reasons, couldn't obtain work at all. As late as 1878 there was again great distress in the city, requiring the not unfamiliar relief programme. All in all, Carlisle had more than its share of hardship during the nineteenth century and it is perhaps surprising that there wasn't more crime there then.

In the meantime, the smaller towns and countryside about it continued to struggle apace with a severe crisis in agriculture as late as 1892. Penrith, some twenty miles to the south, once the seat of almost as much border skirmishing as Carlisle, had developed as a market town, but also had more licensed hostelries than any comparably sized town in the region, with all the accompanying social problems such places brought.

Cockermouth too had experienced its share of fighting in the not too distant past, given that it had declared in no uncertain manner for the Puritans in the Civil War, while distress among its own hand loom weavers had occurred as recently as 1857. True, it retained some standing as a market town and had a viable slate industry. But nothing was ever quite as it seemed, there or anywhere else in nineteenth century Cumberland.

On the other hand, it has to be said too that by the end of the nineteenth century, there had also been a number of social changes beneficial to ordinary folk. These had been slow to materialize but more people now had the vote, many had experienced at least some improvement in their working conditions, while homes were now being built with much more thought for those who were to occupy them. This was as true of Carlisle and district as anywhere else.

Of considerable relevance, drunkenness, the cause of much violent crime in the country as a whole, had also begun to decline towards the end of Victoria's reign. Alcohol abuse would never be totally eradicated anywhere. Carlisle for instance, like Penrith, still had far too many public houses to effect any dramatic change in drinking habits and their inevitable repercussions. Nevertheless, thanks to temperance adherents and others, drinking had undoubtedly diminished in Cumberland as elsewhere, which was no bad thing, and violent crime as a whole did fall notably.

The First World War and its aftermath brought fresh hardship to Carlisle and district as it did everywhere else but gradually the situation began to improve again. Today there is much more money and work in the area plus a whole network of roads to facilitate communication. Unfortunately, this has also tended to bring with it a rise in violent crime, a resurgence of heavy drinking and new kinds of deviance. However, locals are assured that the region is still one of the safest in modern Britain, in spite of its depressed and volatile history.

Carlisle Court buildings and Police Headquarters as they are today. Andrew Richardson

Chapter 1

An Uncontrollable Frenzy
1826

... he snapped, taking out a hammer and beating her about the head ...

Though Carlisle had been a comparatively small place for many years, by the first quarter of the nineteenth century it had spread out beyond the original walls and was continuing to do so. Yet even then, there remained green fields close to the heart of the city itself. It was in one of these fields, in the St Nicholas area that twenty-six year old Mary Brown was discovered dying on Wednesday, 6 September 1826. The young woman had been battered about the head with a blunt instrument to the extent that her brains were protruding. The forefinger of her right hand had been broken in an assumed attempt to ward off the frenzied blows of her assailant. Her clothing was saturated in blood.

It was the first crime of its kind within the city environs that century. Though there was as yet no established police force to call upon, the horrified citizens were not kept long in suspense, the perpetrator himself leading locals to the body of his victim. He was a forty-five year old Irish market trader, Philip Tinnaney, who like many of his countrymen, had came originally to the area in search of work and stayed on. From his emotional babbling both before and at the scene of the crime, a picture soon emerged, to be enlarged upon by those witnesses called to the subsequent inquest.

Everything had apparently come to a violent head the previous day. Mary Brown, if scarcely a courtesan, was not in the opinion of her neighbours and associates, a woman of good character. She and her husband, a Wetheral blacksmith, were parted. Mary had taken a single room the previous year amidst the labyrinth of mean streets lying in and around the St Nicholas area. Impressions are of a woman of easy virtue who liked male company and a good time, but who wasn't prepared to tie herself down to anyone.

Some seven weeks before the tragedy, Philip Tinnaney had taken to visiting her in her room and a close relationship had developed. But

St Nicholas, Carlisle, in 2005, greatly changed since the frenzied Tinnaney murder of 1826. Andrew Richardson

Mary didn't want to live with him and friction began to develop. It was a not unfamiliar situation. While his passion for her continued unabated, she began avoiding him and instructed the landlady to forbid him entry to the house. This infuriated Tinnaney who was given to a weakness for drink and liable to lose control of himself. On the Sunday before the crime he struck Brown in the face. He returned to her lodgings on the Monday and gained entry in an inebriated state, seeking the new man in her life while she hid under the bed. Finding no one, he took off in search of more drink. Nevertheless, he must have won her round again to an extent for the couple were seen together between 2 and 3 pm on the fatal day by a local man, walking towards the field where she was eventually found.

As Tinnaney was to tell it, he was determined to see the far end of her. Yet still apparently hoping to win her back too, he had taken along a bottle of rum in his pocket which he invited her to share. Becoming increasingly drunk, he pleaded with her to accommodate him. When she refused, he snapped, taking out a hammer and beating her about the head in a blind rage before furiously throwing the hammer away. Then suddenly horrified by what he had done, he fled across the River Esk into Scotland and hid in a barn overnight, only to retrace his steps towards Carlisle the following morning. There he took locals to where his victim lay dying. At first she was carried to her lodgings. But then wiser counsels prevailed and the unfortunate woman was removed to the local workhouse. However, despite professional attention, death quickly followed.

In the meantime, the wretched perpetrator, who had informed everyone prepared to listen of his guilt, had been lodged in the city gaol. At an inquest the following day in the *Jovial Butcher Inn*, the jury returned a verdict of wilful murder against him. He remained in custody for the next five months awaiting trial, miserably dejected, scarcely speaking initially, adamant that he wanted to die for his sins.

For company he had a suave individual from West Cumberland, twenty-four year old Robert Fox, though it was doubtful if he had much in common with the stocky farm labourer who had recently disposed of his wife and unborn child with arsenic. What did emerge was that compared with Fox, Tinnaney began to prove remarkably intelligent for one of his class, talking now when it suited him on controversial points of religion. He also proved capable of writing a neat hand. Gradually he became more tranquil and appeared grateful for any kindness shown him, with a prayer book constantly by him.

Finally, in March 1827, came the Spring Assizes. With the fervour of one longing for martyrdom, Tinnaney handed up a poem to the judge, written by himself, which he requested His Lordship to read prior to the commencement of the trial. It was scarcely on a par with the verse of the Lake Poets, but did make its point:

Judgement without mercy, I own is my due
I murdered the woman, my confession is true,
With me you may do as you please,
In your great hands you hold the keys
Of Life or Death
'Tis one request of you I crave
Leave not this corruption in a grave
It would be too great honour on it conferred
Where Christian bodies are interred.

There was more in a similar vein. We do not know if the judge took time to read it all. The verdict was a foregone conclusion in any case, the trial virtually a repetition of the inquest with the same witnesses there to testify to what they had heard and seen. Tinnaney sank slobbering onto his knees as the death sentence was pronounced.

Fox received a like sentence. During the short time left to them, the two men engaged in a final wave of penitential exercises, Tinnaney being however, the more intense and fervent. It was as though he couldn't wait to atone for his crime and this may have been true. Yet he remained an enigma too, clever in his way, drawing constantly upon his devout Catholic upbringing, but like Fox, with a history of dishonesty and dissolution. Fox had deliberately set fire to a former employer's property and had been suspected of an even more serious offence. Tinnaney, though a ribbon seller at the time of his final crime, had also been a jobbing labourer. There was one particular man who had fallen for his glib tongue and given him work, only to be fiercely threatened with a spade for criticizing the poor standard of the work done and fortunate to escape serious injury. More recently, a local woman had fainted upon hearing his lurid description of how he had beaten Mary Brown and hammered her brains out; it were almost as though he derived some twisted satisfaction from constantly going over the event. And he never did express any sympathy for the unfortunate woman as an individual.

He and Fox were to be at least memorable in that they were the first murderers to be hanged on the front wall of the new Carlisle Gaol on 12 March 1827. Tinnaney concluded his devotions on the platform for about eight minutes. Then both men were turned off before a vast multitude, waiting for hours to witness the double spectacle. Fox died slowly, but the Irishman, an incongruous figure in a shabby blue coat and trousers, was to have a much speedier exit, expiring within five minutes.

Chapter 2

A Murky Secret
1877

Meanwhile, back at Penrith, an abominable smell had begun issuing from the storeroom ...

lizabeth Kirkbride was unlike many of the illiterate, poverty-stricken women coming regularly before the courts in nineteenth century Cumberland and elsewhere. She was educated and refined, having been born into a comfortable home in the Liverpool area, the only child of middle class parents. Presently her father retired from his government post and went with his wife to live at Helton, a short distance from Penrith and then situated just over the border in the former county of Westmorland. At first their daughter was not too involved with the region, having made a marriage of her own in the Liverpool area to a prison officer named Kirkbride, where the couple continued to reside with their four sons. However, when the husband suddenly died, his income ended with him. His widow was subsequently thrown onto the goodness of her

Helton today, where Elizabeth Kirkbride had her school. Andrew Richardson

parents and in-laws, who made some attempt to assist. While she and the two elder sons moved in with her parents, Mr and Mrs Hayton, at Helton, the in-laws relieved additional pressure by taking the two younger boys.

This was more generous assistance than many bereaved women with dependent children could have hoped to receive, then or now. Elizabeth Kirkbride did at least attempt to build upon it by seeking an income in her own right, hoping perhaps to make a new home for herself and her sons. Of course there were fewer opportunities for women then, but she was not badly educated to the extent that she apparently spoke several languages. She did not aspire to simply become a governess or a schoolteacher as her mother had been. Indeed, being at that time no more than thirty years of age she aimed higher, opening her own school at Helton.

At a less salubrious level however, she also embarked upon an affair with a dubious individual from nearby Askham, assumed to be already married, which of itself appeared sufficient to keep her occupied in illicit meetings during the evening and early hours at least. Little remains secret too long in a rural community and the widow became a not unfamiliar figure, negotiating the dark country lanes as she travelled to and from the embraces of her lover. There were, no doubt, plenty of knowing smiles and sniggers but she might have continued in this way indefinitely and indeed, the affair continued for some years. But then a further death occurred.

This death was of her father, John Hayton. The impression had always been of a man of means but now it became obvious that he had been less affluent than supposed. His wife too was in worsening health and Elizabeth Kirkbride had the added problem of a failing school, perhaps as a result of all the gossip she had incurred through her personal life. Nothing daunted, in spite of her mother's frailty and insolvency, she moved on to the village of Langwathby, not too far distant, with the intention of opening a new school there, utilizing what capital remained though perhaps beggaring her mother irrevocably in the process. Unfortunately for both women the project failed. Soon too the old lady died and her creditors sold up her remaining effects. At the same time they foreclosed upon the daughter's meagre assets. Everything had begun to fall apart.

The now thoroughly impoverished thirty-nine year old widow faced complete ruin. But though eleven years had now elapsed since her husband's death, she was as yet comparatively young and not unprepossessing, being described as dark, slightly built, well spoken and not unattractive. Was it yet too late? And where was her lover meanwhile? Couldn't he help? In fact he had recently married

Askham village the home of the failed teacher's lover. Andrew Richardson

someone else and there is no evidence that he did anything at all to assist the woman he had finally rejected.

For the moment, the wretched penniless woman had at least been offered a help line by her eldest son, John, now respectably employed back on Merseyside and residing there with a sixteen year old brother. The two young men were only living in rented rooms in the home of a ship steward's wife. But the parlour there was available for Mrs Kirkbride if she wanted it and she accepted, John and his brother taking responsibility for the rent.

First however, the widow appeared especially concerned about some boxes she didn't want to take to Liverpool until she was fully established there. Such thinking appeared reasonable enough and she took it upon herself in June 1876 to approach the landlord of the *Griffin Inn* at Penrith, asking if he would store the boxes until she was settled with her sons in Liverpool. The landlord was happy to oblige and the boxes were placed in a storeroom at the inn. Thereupon Mrs Kirkbride continued on her way to Liverpool and arrived at her new abode with the minimum of luggage and not appearing too composed.

However, she presently appeared more relaxed following the arrival of two large trunks from Aintree where she had been recently visiting. These were placed upstairs on a landing though remained unopened.

Over subsequent months, the widow remained much of the time in her room doing needlework, but the landlady began to notice that certain articles had begun to go missing from the house: a coat, a tablecloth and a blanket. She felt she knew who the culprit was but held fire for the moment.

Meanwhile, back at Penrith, an abominable smell had begun issuing from the storeroom at the *Griffin Inn*. This was traced to one of the boxes left there by the widow the previous summer and still unclaimed though it was now January 1877. The landlord felt he had no choice but to open the box, never imagining what he would find. There lay the body of a decomposing child. It was fully developed with a woman's garter encircling its neck, indicating strangulation. It appeared to have been dead for some time. Another box was opened and the remains of another child were revealed in an advanced state of decay, albeit with sufficient evidence left to reveal crude attempts to cut its throat. By this time the smell had became overpowering. The landlord lost no time in contacting the police. The widow's address was available and she was visited by police officers on the Saturday following the discovery of the tragic remains at Penrith. The policemen found Elizabeth Kirkbride in the house alone. She denied everything but agreed to accompany them back to Penrith, only requesting that a note be left for her sons playing things down for the moment. The request was acceded to and the party left the house.

The following Monday morning, the landlady, Mrs Obeti, realized that her female lodger whom she had never trusted had gone. The missing articles had still never been accounted for and the landlady became thoroughly incensed. She determined to have the matter out with John Kirkbride when he returned for lunch. Embarrassed, the young fellow could only explain that his mother had been called back to Penrith on unknown business but had no qualms about offering some books and glasses in lieu of the goods missing from the house, the implication being that he trusted his mother no more than the landlady did. When Mrs Obeti said that the books and glasses weren't enough, John Kirkbride went upstairs and prised open one of the trunks, leaving the landlady to help herself while he returned to work.

The trunk was carried down into the yard. The same over-powering smell began to assail Mrs Obeti as had assailed the landlord of the *Griffin Inn*, as she threw back the lid and began to sort through the contents. Packed among clothes and carpets were no fewer than three corpses of newly born children in varying stages of decomposition, one with string tied around its neck. Another child was headless, though the head was found at the bottom of the trunk. If the trunk had not been opened, the remains could have remained there indefinitely given that the lid had been so tightly sealed down. Not unnaturally, the Liverpool landlady reacted as the landlord at Penrith had done. Filled with horror and disgust, she called in the police.

As matters had evolved, Elizabeth Kirkbride was still in Liverpool, undergoing questioning about the contents of the boxes at Penrith. Up to now she had revealed nothing but when confronted with Mrs Obeti's discovery, finally proceeded to make a confession of sorts. Ambiguous as ever, she continued to deny having murdered any of the children though no one had even accused her of that as yet. What she did now reveal was her former lover's name as well as his occupation and address: Thomas Moss, tea, ham and bacon dealer of Askham, near Penrith. Moss, she claimed, was to blame for her entire predicament. He was the only man she had had anything to do with since her widowhood, promising to marry her when he was free to do so. But instead, he had married someone else. This however was the extent of her statement.

The woman's bitterness was understandable in its way, and she might well have hoped that Moss would now join her in custody. But for some reason, the man was never approached. Neither did he ever come forward to admit or deny his involvement, though did take the precaution of having a solicitor in court to represent his interests as necessary. In the event, the solicitor was never called upon to do anything, though possibly his client could have gone some way towards clearing up a number of remaining anomalies.

Nevertheless, the police still appeared to have plenty to go on. No sooner had the widow made her short statement than her son, William, revealed that he thought there might be yet another body, buried under a pear tree at Helton. Such proved to be the case, with the son claiming to recall seeing his mother at work with a spade there some six years previously.

Limited though overall knowledge of anatomy and physiology remained in 1877, there had been some advances. Therefore it was possible to date the latest corpse as being no more than a few years old, which fitted in with what the youth had said to an extent. It had also been possible to roughly date most of the other decomposing bodies. Of those in the trunk, one had been there around ten years, the decapitated body eight years, and the one best preserved for perhaps five years. Of the bodies discovered at Penrith, one was difficult to assess because of decomposition, but it was thought that the other had been hidden away no more than two years.

All in all, the corpses evidenced a period of around ten years continuous adultery. Ostensibly, this was deemed to be disgraceful by the Victorian public. Of greater concern however, was the garter discovered around the neck of one of the children at Penrith. This and the crude attempt to cut the throat of a second, plus the piece of string around the neck of a third, was surely proof of more than the standard act of a single concealment by single parents, not uncommon in the region and beyond it.

But though the small shabby woman in black no doubt realized she might well be in serious trouble, she retained her composure and kept her own counsel, even while the train bringing her back under escort to Penrith was besieged at every station by abusive crowds. Penniless and embittered, with her former lover remaining off the scene and her family having all but disowned her, she might well have wondered if life was even worth living? Meanwhile, many following the case anticipated that she would surely go the way of Maria Manning, Catherine Wilson, and other notorious Victorian murderesses.

But in fact, such was not to be. Given the vagaries then attending any case of concealment of birth, the public ought to have known better. The end of the affair was a feeble anti-climax in spite of the earlier outcry, with all its accompanying evidence of guilt. For Elizabeth Kirkbride still had more going for her than Manning, Wilson and their ilk. Though it had indeed been possible to roughly assess the ages of the tiny corpses, no one amongst the medical fraternity was yet prepared to swear that any of the children had not already been born dead. Therefore the widow was eventually found guilty of concealment of birth only, like many others of her poorer compatriots during the period. In the end she received a mere twenty-seven months imprisonment, in spite of the evidence that some attempt could have been made to silence at least three of the children beforehand.

Gradually the whole sorry business became yesterday's news, the public as a whole feeling let down but perhaps considering that it was best forgotten after all. This may be one of the reasons why the case eventually became relegated to comparative obscurity.

Chapter 3

Execution of an Earl
1323

He was allowed to hang for a few moments before being cut down, still alive.

Despite a lack of documentation relating to medieval Carlisle and the region about it, there is still sufficient material to provide us with a reasonable picture to work from. The barbaric execution of Andrew de Harcla in 1323 is an example of such.

Harcla first came to prominence when, as captain of Carlisle Castle, he organized a spirited ten-day defence of the city against Robert Bruce in 1315 which saw the Scots humbled and driven off. Following this he rose rapidly in the esteem of the reigning monarch, Edward II. A charter quickly materialized, granting Carlisle considerable economic favours, accompanied by a flattering vignette adorned with Harcla's likeness atop one of the castle's towers, surrounded by gallant Carlisle citizens and beyond the wall, a Scot pierced through by a spear.

The city's captain was also granted custody of land as far south as Lancashire. In 1321–22 he captured Thomas, Earl of Lancaster, who along with other English dissidents had gone over to the Scots. Nor was he averse to accusing another nobleman, Robert de Wulseley, of bearing arms against Edward, falsely as it appeared, and seizing his lands. Shortly afterwards, he was made Earl of Carlisle. His career appeared unstoppable. Then suddenly everything began to go wrong for him.

We shall never know all the background dynamics. What we do know is that Robert Bruce returned with his army to Cumberland in 1322 and swept south as far as Lancashire, burning Rose Castle en route. He returned via Beaumont, no more than four miles south of Carlisle, and committed further atrocities while encamped there. Harcla appeared unable to do a great deal to check the Scottish

Carlisle Castle, still ostensibly grim and formidable, where Andrew de Harcla was arrested and tried for high treason in 1323. Andrew Richardson

marauders in this instance, presumably because he was short of men and resources. Instead, he made a treaty with Bruce who returned to Scotland unmolested.

The monarch was duly concerned when he heard of this and in January 1323, summoned Harcla to give him an explanation. The former favourite declined to appear. Consequently, Lord Lucy, Sheriff of Cumberland, was ordered to arrest the errant earl without delay. Harcla appeared curiously supine; he made no opposition to Lucy entering the castle with an accompanying entourage, weapons concealed under their cloaks, apparently accepting that they were there on a courtesy visit. He was arrested in his quarters, while the guards at the gates were then compelled to lay down their arms.

Events moved swiftly thereafter. On 3 March 1323, charged with high treason and of making a treaty with the Scots, Harcla was tried in the castle before Sir Gudfrid de Scrope, the chief judge. Found guilty, it was ordered that following the confiscation of his sword and spurs, he was to be dragged by horses to the gallows on Harraby Hill, there to be hung, drawn and quartered.

Upon hearing this dread pronouncement, Harcla is said to have been unmoved, merely replying that though they might divide his body at their pleasure, he commended his soul to God. There followed a grim procession from the castle and through the city with its wooden houses and gaping crowds. The doomed man remained composed as he was dragged along behind a team of horses, hands clasped above him and eyes uplifted to the sky. The grim procession passed through the English gate and down what is now Botchergate, along London Road and up onto Harraby Hill, better known in these times as Chertsey Mount.

Once relieved of his shackles, the former earl stood up, erect and dignified. He explained in clear tones why he had made the treaty with the Scots though his words appeared to fall on deaf ears. Then the rope went around his neck. He was allowed to hang for a few moments before being cut down, still alive. Then he was disembowelled, and his entrails burnt in a brazier before his eyes. Throughout his horrific ordeal, the condemned man remained stoical. Finally, his head was mercifully struck from his body with an axe and his still warm carcase cut into quarters. The parts were afterwards displayed at Carlisle, Newcastle, York and Shrewsbury, with the head spiked on London Bridge.

So ended the life and career of a man obviously well endowed with courage though not averse to self-seeking either, but perhaps genuinely forced into doing what he had done in this instance. There is no mention of a wife but his remains were later gathered together and given to his sister Sarah for proper burial.

Even then, Andrew de Harcla continued to be mentioned in the official calendar of the times for several years as his land and possessions were divided up. He was invariably referred to as 'the late rebel' and was even accused of carrying away vital stores after adhering to the Scottish enemy.

In a way he does remain something of an enigmatic figure while engendering a measure of sympathy, given that Edward II had himself been seeking peace with the Scots before Harcla entered into full negotiation with them. Furthermore, a short time following the earl's execution, Edward concluded such a peace in his own right, though it was not long afterwards before he too was toppled by those dissatisfied with his qualities of leadership, suffering an even more horrific death than Harcla in Berkeley Castle.

Chapter 4

A Double Murder at Longburn
1808

In the light of the flickering candle, he saw that one of her fingers had been almost cut off...

ames Wood was a native of then burgeoning Carlisle where, like many more, he had trained as a weaver. We are handicapped in that we do not know his age, nor do we have a physical description of him. A witness at his trial, a Mr Stamp, called upon by the defence to tender a few favourable words, stated that three or four years previously the prisoner, when a boy, was employed under him, albeit adding that his knowledge of him was so exceedingly scanty, not knowing him by name previous to his being apprehended, that he was unable to say anything positive in his favour!

From this we can at least deduce that the wretch could have been no more than nineteen or twenty years of age at the time of his later villainy and that he may have cut at best, an insignificant figure altogether as a boy. However, given that just a few years afterwards, he had been partially employed doing hard manual work on the farm of his victims, and the untrammelled violence of his crimes there, he might well have developed into a much more positive and robust individual.

Be this as it may, when he first arrived at Longburn in the parish of Bromfield, situated some miles west of Carlisle on the Solway Plain where Thomas Smith lived with his wife, Margaret and her sister, Jane Pattinson, he was in needy straits, advising that though a trained weaver with parents in Carlisle, more recently he had deserted from His Majesty's Navy after being impressed on board a man-of-war and was effectively on the run. Being possessed of little more than the clothes he stood up in he required work, though appeared to have had little success in the area to date.

The parish of Longburn, scene of James Wood's despicable crime. Andrew Richardson

This was scarcely surprising, given that he had been tramping around one of the more remote Cumbrian regions primarily given over to small farms. But Thomas Smith was a trained weaver himself, working from home. It was his wife and sister-in-law who usually attended to the farm. He promptly hired Wood as a journeyman weaver, with secondary duties on the farm as necessary. He wasn't greatly concerned that the youth was a deserter. Few had much time for the press gangs.

At first all went well and Wood quickly became more like a son within the elderly household. He was charged seven shillings a week for his board but could make fifteen shillings a week weaving. Yet though a good workman, he appeared lazy, gradually slackening off until he rarely made more than seven shillings. He therefore remained poor but didn't complain. He may have begun to feel covetous however, eyeing the money kept in the house, while having to borrow five shillings simply to buy a pair of clogs.

Matters came all too quickly to a head. Wood had arrived in November 1807. The following year, on 19 January, Thomas Smith set off for Wigton Market with his cloth, a journey he made regularly, leaving Wood alone with the two women as usual. Perhaps of greater significance, there was a sum in excess of £7 also left at home in this instance, a huge amount of money in 1808. It was in a cash box in the parlour. Margaret Smith had the key.

The old weaver enjoyed a good day's trading, returning home in the gloom of a wet winter evening. He was surprised to find the cattle still out in the yard and the whole place shrouded in silence. Upon entering the house he discovered his sister-in-law sitting on a chair with her head lying on the table. She was still alive but silent. Smith assumed in his innocence that she had had a fall and that his wife and Wood had gone for medical assistance. At that time he observed only a wound on the woman's forehead.

He attended to the wailing cattle for a few minutes, then returned and lit a candle. He found that his sister-in-law had fallen forward into a pool of blood. In the light of the flickering candle, he saw that one of her fingers had been almost cut off and that there was a huge wound on her head. Now realizing that there must have been foul play he began seeking desperately for his wife, finding her lying in the barn with her skull cracked. Next he discovered the cash box broken open and all its contents missing. Beside it lay a billhook saturated with blood. Of James Wood there remained no sign.

The distraught weaver called in his nearest neighbours. They sought to revive Margaret Smith but within an hour, both she and her sister were dead. There appeared to be only one culprit but where was he? In 1808 the organized forces of law and order were comparatively negligible. It was a younger relative of the two victims, John Bell, who took it upon himself to pursue Wood. On the strength of a tip-off, he made directly for Wigton. Obtaining no result there, he rode across the Solway Plain to Bowness and took a boat over the estuary to Scotland, finally running the wanted man to earth at Cumertrees, between Annan and Dumfries, a not unremarkable achievement.

Wood was willing to talk, saying he had left Longburn Farm because three ruffians had arrived to arrest him. When Bell enquired if the ruffians had hurt Margaret and Jane the youth had no answer. He was taken before a magistrate and put in the local prison where he was searched. Much of the stolen money came to light. Also hidden in his hat was an expensive watch, which it transpired he had recently purchased in Annan. The suspected man undertook to dictate a confession, stating that he had killed the womenfolk before breaking open the cash box, albeit emphasizing that he had killed Margaret Smith with a flail and not the billhook. That night he was returned south and lodged in Carlisle Gaol.

By the time of his trial the following August, he had undergone a change of mind again, saying he had left the two women alive in the house when he departed on the morning of 19 January. This was of course true in part, but they had died soon enough following the battering they had received. The prosecution had several valid points to make in its turn. Hadn't the accused already made a confession without being forced to do so, and even requested a significant alteration to it? And if confronted by three ruffians, why hadn't he alerted neighbours if he had thought the two women were also in danger? Instead he had gone off drinking and dancing! Then when apprehended, he had initially attempted to conceal the stolen money as well as the watch. There was more in this vein after which it took the jury only a few minutes to find James Wood guilty of robbery and double murder. He was hanged shortly afterwards on Carlisle Sands, praying for forgiveness.

Chapter 5

Two Juvenile Offenders 1830

... they were to claim they were both threatened with violence if they didn't confess.

The offence committed by Robert Lamb, fifteen years old, and Joseph Furnace, thirteen, would scarcely be termed a foul deed in these times. Like thousands of others of their kind in nineteenth century Cumberland, they would now be considered fairly minor offenders. Yet their crime was considered serious enough to merit the death penalty and according to one local book, both were hanged at Carlisle in March 1830 for housebreaking. Foul deeds could cover a very wide range of offending in those days.

Nevertheless, the author of the book did get it wrong in this instance. The twosome weren't hanged. However, they could have been. By stealing from a dwelling house they were committing what was still a capital offence in 1830. But if every offender, juvenile or otherwise, had been hanged at Carlisle, or anywhere else in the British Isles, during or before that period, there would not have been enough hangmen available. The authorities had become subtler than that; they chose to make examples. Cumberland as a whole had as good a record as any in this respect.

The likes of Lamb and Furnace would have been the last to merit capital punishment by 1830. Where the author got his 'facts' from is purely academic now. What their case still illustrates however, is that the punishment they did receive was no soft option. Perhaps surprisingly, there were also those who were acquitted in those days, but most could still expect to be dealt with severely, more so if property was involved.

Lamb and Furnace were two such examples. Both were from lowly backgrounds, both were illiterate. Lamb was a chimney sweep. Furnace had no regular employment. They appeared with a nineteen year old companion, Charles Linton, at the Cumberland Lent Assizes on 6 March 1830. All three were indicted for having feloniously stolen and carried away from the dwelling house of George Stuart of Townhead, Penrith, five sheets, two shirts, one child's hat, two bolster slips, one silver watch and other articles in August 1829. Undoubtedly, it is true, a longer list of stolen property than was generally the norm.

The crime had been made easier by the fact that Stuart was a hawker and often absent from home. But the theft was discovered quickly enough and Lamb was questioned. He admitted that he had cut up the sheets and sold them off as rags. He may also have implicated Furnace for both were soon in the local House of Correction where they were to claim they were both threatened with violence if they didn't confess. Subsequently, they owned up, though later denied the offence. It was too late. Their character witness failed to materialize and they had no defence counsel. Linton, possibly a receiver of the ill-gotten gains, shrewdly said nothing and as a result, was acquitted!

Thereupon the judge delivered an extensive lecture, advising the two reprobates that they had both been convicted on the clearest evidence, independent of their own voluntary confession, of a very serious crime, which the law authorized to be punished by death. They had caused considerable aggravation and robbed a poor man. But as it was, he would now only order judgement of death to be

Townhead, Penrith, scene of the crime of the two unfortunate juveniles, Lamb and Furnace, leading to judgement of death. Andrew Richardson

recorded against them, recommending them instead to the merciful consideration of His Majesty the King, who he hoped would be graciously pleased to assign them a lighter punishment.

This was so much legal flummery. The reigning monarch, George IV, already had a much more unsavoury reputation than the two wretched Penrith delinquents would ever have and would never know of their existence. The Learned Judge simply had to go through this ritual prior to passing sentence.

Seeing Lamb as the principal offender who had seduced the other unfortunate youth, he ordered him to be transported, thereby conferring in his opinion, a great benefit on society, bearing in mind that few ever returned from down under. He then dealt with Furnace, making much play on the fact that he had a certificate testifying to the previous good character of the thirteen year old, who was still young and not, he hoped, beyond improvement.

Nonetheless, the sentence meted out in this instance was scarcely one to uplift the anxious boy before him. He too would be shipped out but sent on board a penitentiary ship for the term of his transportation where he might be taught a trade and be returned a more useful member of society. No specific trade was mentioned nor time limit given and considering the conditions prevailing at sea in those days, it is scarcely surprising that Furnace wept bitterly prior to being launched roughly into a world far removed from the small market town where he had grown up.

Lamb appeared far less fazed, possibly reasoning in his ignorance that he might even be given the opportunity to mine for gold in the land where he was headed for, though this appeared unlikely.

Such was the standard way of dealing with most juvenile offenders in 1830 in Carlisle and beyond, and would continue to be for some decades to come.

Chapter 6

Murder Most Foul
1860

... it emerged that the victim and the husbandman had not always been on good terms.

From time to time in the annals of murder there occur dark deeds attaining a much higher profile than others of their kind. Such was the case in the killing of a maidservant, Ann Sewell, by the oafish hired man, George Cass, at Beckhouse Farm in March 1860. At the time, this crime was reported nationwide in all its stages: the discovery of the body, the police investigation, the arrest of the killer and his confession, the trial and execution. Added interest was afforded by the fact that the crime took place in a lonely and beautiful part of the county, yet within a fairly short distance of both Cockermouth and Carlisle, namely the Vale of Embleton.

The murder scene is little changed today. Unless the visitor is well instructed beforehand, he or she may find it difficult to locate the hamlet of Beckhouse, being as it is little more than a collection of farmhouses and their adjacent buildings, a church and a shed where the parish hearse was formerly kept. Beckhouse Farm is situated a short distance from the church up a narrow lane; it appears to have almost stood still in time, like everything about it. If George Cass were to somehow reappear in leggings and cord breeches leading his horse, he would blend perfectly into the tranquil scene as though he had never been away.

The morning of 26 March 1860 was as normal as any within the rural community. At Beckhouse Farm the proprietor, Thomas Fearon, was about to take his widowed mother, Isabella, to Cockermouth Market before attending to other business. Mother and son set off, leaving their husbandman, twenty-four year old George Cass and two day labourers, James Eland and James Boak, to get on with their work in the fields. The house was left in charge of the twenty-six year old servant girl, Ann Sewell.

Beckhouse Farm today, still peacefully situated, but where one of the most brutal murders in the region took place. Andrew Richardson

It was a fine dry morning. Before long, the Embleton parish clerk, John Robinson, was knocking on the farmhouse door to borrow a mop and pail from the not unattractive maidservant. His hearse had been splashed with mud the day before and he wanted to wash and polish it. At noon, Ann served dinner to Cass, Eland, Boak, and three men from Keswick, who had called to collect a load of grain ordered by their employer. The atmosphere was cordial as everyone had their say and Eland teased Sewell about a meeting they had had the evening before at the *Blue Bell Inn*. But by 2 pm, the men had all returned to work and the servant girl prepared to clean the fireplace.

This was the last time she was seen alive except by the man who killed her. When John Robinson returned at 3.30 pm. to hand in the mop and pail, he found the house silent and locked up and though he knocked loudly there was no reply. He also observed Cass's horse in the stable but though this seemed odd, he didn't feel there was anything to be particularly concerned about and returned across the field to the church, assuming that the girl herself would be out among the livestock.

When Isabella Fearon returned at 5 pm. she found the farmhouse still locked up and silent. Given that Ann Sewell was prone to fainting fits, she felt the girl might be lying inside in a swoon and recruited a neighbour's maidservant, Sarah Earle, to climb through a window and investigate. What Sarah discovered left her deeply shocked.

Ann Sewell lay face down in a pool of blood in the passageway, a kitchen knife in her left hand. The girl retreated back through the window to Mrs Fearon and the alarm was raised. Cass, discovered working in a nearby field, was advised of the situation. He leapt onto his horse and rode bareback to the farm, meeting up with a neighbour, Joseph Clarke, who suggested they enter the house.

Cass declined to enter through the window but advised that he could open the kitchen door by a method he used whenever he returned late. He removed a piece of iron from the farmhouse eaves and easily opened the door. Clarke entered with the two women while Cass went off to seek other assistance. The trio discovered that the girl's throat was so violently slashed that the spinal cord had been completely severed. Their first assumption was that she had committed suicide. It was Cass who again galloped off to alert the police and coroner, crying that the young woman had cut her throat.

In 1860, detection as a science still had some way to go. But there was a new, far-seeing man who had recently succeeded in completely reorganizing the local police forces with some success. This was Chief Constable John Dunne and he immediately took a personal interest in the case. It became apparent that Ann Sewell couldn't have taken her own life. Her wound was too severe; besides, she had been right-handed and the knife had been found in her left hand. But, of equal relevance, Cass had proved he could manipulate the locked door. And it emerged that the victim and the husbandman had not always been on good terms. Dunne quickly reached the conclusion that George Cass could be the culprit.

On the other hand, there had been other men on the scene that day too. For a time Eland was under suspicion, more so since he had recently been making up to Sewell and had a prison record. John Robinson also fell under a cloud, and the victim's boy friend, John Farrish. But gradually they were all eliminated. That still left Cass.

Sir John Dunne, Chief Constable of Cumberland and Westmorland, who never really doubted the identity of the Beckhouse killer. Cumbria Police

A fortnight passed but no arrest was made, for definite proof was yet required. Though Cass had proved that he could enter the house at will and also secure the door behind him without a key, he had continued to deny any knowledge of the crime. Neither had any blood been discovered on his clothing and fingerprinting had yet to come into its own. It was true that he and the maidservant had had rows and he had called her a lazy bitch and threatened her on occasions. But there were also those to affirm that the twosome had generally got on well enough and that the girl had been dissatisfied with her place at Beckhouse Farm, not because of Cass, but because she had disliked the lack of social life there. Certainly the hired man, though the son of respectable working people, was seen as bad-tempered, with a predilection for strong drink. However, there were many like him around. He had explained the horse's presence in the stable on the day of the murder by advising that he had been mending his harrow, and had put the flighty animal inside until he completed the task.

Yet still Dunne, and his officers, remained sure Cass was the culprit. Their suspicions were added to by the fact that there was some likelihood the victim had been robbed. And Cass, almost perpetually broke, had had more money to spend of late. On 6 April 1860 they finally acted. George Cass was arrested and went along surprisingly quietly. He was placed in a police cell at Cockermouth and within a short space of time, had dictated a confession. Questions were to be asked as to the methods used to persuade him to do this but it would seem that a solitary session in custody had finally been sufficient to exercise his mind.

What he said essentially was that he had been in the orchard righting a sheep when Ann Sewell wanted him to do something with her clog caulkers. When he declined, she began to verbally abuse him and threw a knife at him in the passageway, catching him in the face. He threw it back and it stuck in her throat. She had then asked him to do away with her. He didn't want to but she begged him and he cut her twice across the neck and she dropped and said no more. He then went into the kitchen after putting the knife in her hand to wash the blood from his waistcoat and hands. He heard Robinson at the door and remained silent. Then he left by a window and taking his horse from the stable, returned to work. That night he searched the dead girl's bedroom for money he'd lent her and took her purse containing £1 6s 4d. He concluded with an apology for what he'd done.

The anomalies in the foregoing are obvious. There was no way that a woman with a knife in her throat could engage anyone in conversation and, in any case, there was no such wound. Nor had she ever appeared the suicidal type. What reason would she have had for taking her own life? It also appeared clear that Cass had robbed her at the time of the murder, though might have been unwilling to admit this, feeling it would further lessen his chances of escaping the noose. The reference to the caulkers was more puzzling; the victim's clogs were discovered to be perfectly sound. But there had been a hammer and a pair of pincers on the kitchen table. Cass was also to claim that friends had taken away his bloodstained clothing. But who were those friends? These matters were never fully explored. Needless to say, he had dictated enough to hang him. Though he later retracted this earlier statement, he was duly found guilty and executed at Carlisle before a crowd of several thousand on 17 August 1860.

Motive for the murder remained obscure but may have had a sexual component. It was known that on a number of occasions, Cass had attempted to sweetheart Sewell but invariably she rejected him. A not unintelligent young woman, she also had a ready tongue and may well have taunted him on that final day to her detriment, goading an insecure, volatile individual to do what he did, when he had merely slipped quietly into the farmhouse after stabling the horse to make a simple pass at her, as he did imply in a final statement. There was certainly evidence of a struggle in the passageway but being stocky and well made, he was the stronger and it had to be soon over, though here we are merely entering the realms of assumption.

Meanwhile, the young woman who had only intended to remain at Beckhouse for six months is still there, buried in the local churchyard, her grave marked by a stone paid for by public subscription. But the stone is now sadly worn and the grave long unattended.

Chapter 7

Dead in a Field
1875

A close examination further established that the skull was extensively fractured on the left side ...

Given the number of single girls in Cumberland disposing of their unwanted offspring in derelict buildings, ditches and anywhere else remotely convenient, there was often some poor wretch in court charged with murder, manslaughter or, at best, concealment of birth. None was as notorious as the widow of Helton, but they still weren't averse to resorting to desperate measures when forced. Cumberland and neighbouring Westmorland outstripped even London by the middle of the nineteenth century for illegitimate births per head of population, with only Norfolk in competition.

A number of reasons have been postulated for this: cultural norms, remote farms employing bored, uneducated girls, cramped accommodation. Maybe, but the reasons are still not totally clear either. Many of the women involved weren't necessarily so unworldly and ignorant by the nineteenth century. Nor were they all living in isolated, restricted circumstances in country or in town. Be this as it may. What was clearer was the plight a single woman could be in anywhere if she did fall pregnant, there being no official birth control in what was, by and large, a hypocritical society. There was no welfare provision either and if a father refused to accept responsibility or the woman's immediate family turned her away, the future might well be one of miserable deprivation for mother and child, hence the number of infants being disposed of at birth.

Liz Armstrong was a not untypical example of this kind of person. Like many of her contemporaries, the twenty year old girl was employed on a lonely farm, in this instance in the Lanercost area. She was only half-educated and without direct support, though had been astute enough to conceal that fact that she was pregnant. When she complained of feeling unwell and wanting to go home for a while, her master gave her a sovereign and sent her on her way shortly before

Easter 1875. She departed, but was back within days, appearing much relieved and continuing with her duties as though nothing had ever been amiss.

In the event, she was not to escape so easily. She had been observed on 20 March by an innkeeper, sitting late by the roadside near Kircambeck where her aunt lived, before heading down towards a stream. The man must have become suspicious because this led to a police constable making a search of the area. He soon found the afterbirth of a child in the River Cambeck. This led to a confrontation between himself and Liz Armstrong in her employer's house. The policeman asked her bluntly if she had given birth to a child, which she denied. Not satisfied, he took her in charge; no sooner had she been cautioned than she said she had given birth to a dead child near her aunt's house.

The body of a female child was found in the field, wrapped in an apron under a covering of clay and leaves. The tiny corpse was taken to Brampton for medical examination on 3 April. The strings of the apron had been tied tightly round its neck twice. A close examination further established that the skull was extensively fractured on the left side and the entire surface of the brain covered with blood. Blood was also discovered in the cavities of the brain. The lungs were in better condition. Though not completely expanded with air, they floated in

The River Cambeck. Andrew Richardson

water; they also floated when they were cut into pieces; they floated with the heart and made a crackling sound.

All these facts convinced the medical men that the infant had breathed fully after birth and that cause of death had therefore to be the damage to the head. Nevertheless, they also felt that if the child's death had been caused by pressure from the apron strings, appearances would have remained much the same. Liz Armstrong appeared to be in serious trouble. There could be no question of her returning to the farm. She was remanded to Carlisle Gaol until the Summer Assizes, charged with wilful murder.

She appeared before Mr Justice Archibald the following July. Almost at once, her defence counsel, Elliot, submitted that there was no case to go to the jury. The judge could not entirely agree but did feel that there must be something more than the evidence available for the jury to safely convict the defendant of murder, even while he continued to feel that there remained some evidence of such. However, he emphasized that there remained the matter of concealment of birth; serious of itself.

Elliot was swiftly on his feet again, contending that the charge of concealment was also in doubt, given the girl's earlier statement that someone else had hidden the body. Given such doubt about her having concealed the corpse, he invited the jury to acquit her, even while she had named no names.

Mr Justice Archibald remained not unsympathetic. He reiterated that it would be unsafe for the jury to bring in a verdict of guilty against the mother for the murder of her child. Nevertheless, in the matter of concealment of birth, the case must be seen in a different light. The hiding of the dead body of a child was indecent, immoral and against the law and he appeared to feel that Liz Armstrong was fully responsible. The jury listened carefully and found the mother guilty of concealment of birth. The sentence was one of twelve months imprisonment with hard labour.

There were those who probably remained convinced that Liz Armstrong was guilty of more than concealment. However, she was one of many and while there were a majority who were to wish the widow of Helton to receive the ultimate sentence two years later, given her persistent whoring and dissembling, she was seen as a gentlewoman who ought to have known better. Liz, like many of her kind in Cumberland and beyond, was seen more as a victim of circumstances and engendered much more sympathy within and outside the courtroom. Her likes could occasionally expect a period of imprisonment though there is no record of any of them ever paying the ultimate penalty.

Chapter 8

An Emotive Affair
1819

Judge Jonathan Raine ... assured the pathetic man that not the slightest gleam of mercy could be held out to him.

hough the number of executions in Cumberland was not excessive during the nineteenth century as compared with other regions, there were still sufficient to excite the attention of the public. We can probably assume that they had little sympathy for most of those who were turned off, even enjoying the spectacle. Yet the execution of Christopher Gale and John Townshend at Carlisle in April 1819 appears to have been badly received by the majority of Cumbrians. It may have helped spearhead the long campaign for the abolition of capital punishment throughout Britain. Some might even have argued that in this instance, the foul deed was perpetrated by the powers-that-be.

Gale, the first of the pair, was comparatively young, the father of three children when he offended. Totally illiterate, he had, nevertheless, proved capable of holding down a job for eleven years as a mail carrier at Cockermouth. Now in March 1819, he appeared at Cumberland Spring Assizes charged with abstracting two bills to a total value of £150 from the mailbag entrusted to his custody between Maryport and Cockermouth on 9 January 1819.

We can but continue to wonder at his state of mind at the time. Being illiterate, he had blandly requested aid in cashing the bills from an innkeeper, Liz Martindale, and then from another individual, Joseph Millican. These involved huge amounts of money which he must surely have realized, if in his right senses, he could never have justified as being his. The innkeeper and Millican, who had had the benefit of some education, both recognized that something was amiss, Millican promptly bringing the matter to the attention of the authorities. Yet despite the weight of detrimental evidence, Gale persisted in saying that a man had given him the notes wrapped in brown paper near Dovenby, even while he had given a totally different version of events to Martindale.

At his trial he declined to say anything in his defence though a character witness described him as having always been an honest man. Notwithstanding, the jury found him guilty without retiring from the box. Judge Jonathan Raine promptly pronounced sentence of death and assured the pathetic man that not the slightest gleam of mercy could be held out to him.

John Townshend was forty-three years old and the father of six children. He had offended some miles distant at Whitehaven but, given that his offending and fate have always been linked to those of Gale, the two appearing at the same court on not dissimilar charges and, being hanged together, he is also given coverage here.

Townshend was indicted for uttering and publishing as true, a forged order and certificate for receipt of prize money due to Mary Hutchinson, sister of Isaac Banks, a deceased mariner. Being in a position of some responsibility he had applied for the prize money on her behalf, albeit resorting to forged signatures and then claimed nothing had been received, while paying the woman at intervals from his own pocket. Banks had been due £31 11s 4d which it was claimed had been sent. Townshend alleged that he had only ever received £18 6s 0d but had paid this out in two instalments of £5 and £13 6s 0d to the applicant, not being able to pay it when first asked. He had utilized the money for his own use but paid it back, while doggedly denying that anything additional had ever been received. He too was sentenced to death and promptly burst into tears.

Of course both men had done wrong and the offence was serious enough. But in Gale's case, the stolen bills had been quickly recovered, and Townshend was always to maintain that he had paid back all the money he had obtained through his ill-considered action. Certainly those were harsher times, and Townshend may have been lying. But it was still felt by many that the offences merited, if anything, a spell of transportation rather than the death penalty, which had only once been carried out for forgery locally since 1800, and never for theft since well before then.

No sooner had the death sentences been pronounced than some attempt was, at least, made to save the situation. Petitions were set in train as far away as Lancaster and Whitehaven but alas, these efforts ought to have come into play sooner. The religious fraternity for their part were concerned as usual to at least save the souls of the offenders. They achieved a measure of success with Townshend, a thinking man of some education. Indeed, he was said to be of

SOME PARTICULARS

RELATIVE TO

John Townshend

AND

CHRISTOPHER GALE,

Previous to, and at the Place of Execution.

THESE two unfortunate men had been capitally convicted at the Cumberland Commission of Assize in March, 1819, before Mr. Commissioner Raine—TOWNSHEND of forging Signatures for the payment of Seamen's Prize Money, and GALE of robbing the Mail, of which he was the carrier, between Maryport and Cockermouth ; the facts relative to which were clearly made out against both the prisoners ; one of whom is the father of three, and the other of six children, who will thus, by the tragical end of their parents, be thrown destitute upon the world.

Townshend was a man of some education, though by no means to that extent which has generally been represented. He seems to have been in the habit of at least occasional attendance on public worship ; and he has repeatedly mentioned the names of some clergymen whose faithful preaching he can now well remember ; but which at the time, alas ! he did not improve. Since his condemnation he had employed much of his time in writing, and altogether on religious subjects. The prayers which he has written are indeed not very correctly expressed, yet they certainly indicate a good share of religious knowledge, and a deep impression of sacred truth.—We are informed by some of his visitors, that they have been much affected and pleased with his extempore prayers, as well as his Christian conversation in general. His conduct too, as far as we can learn, had been throughout very becoming: and we trust that the compassionate Deity has answered the numerous petitions on his behalf, in the salvation of his soul.

It would have been gratifying could we have been able to present a similar statement of his fellow-prisoner. But Gale, it seems, was still the same character : unmoved and unimpressed by any circumstance from the period of his first apprehension to the last, he continued to betray the same stupidity and uncommon indifference. He could neither write nor read, and therefore it may be expected that his ignorance was excessive : but he has had ample means of instruction, and were he *perfectly rational*, some alteration must have been produced. How such a degree of continued insensibility is to be accounted for, we confess ourselves ignorant ; and whether it can be attributed to any thing else than partial idiocy we must leave for others to determine. Our best wish for this unfortunate convict is, that since he has forfeited his life, he may have " mercy of the Lord unto eternal life."

Through the medium of an intimate friend of his, at the request of the unhappy J. Townshend, we communicate, as under, his last public declaration :—

" My ever dear Sir—It is my request that I make known to the world prior to my suffering the sentence of the law, which awaits me to-morrow, that I have no hidden secrets to suppress whatever ; neither do I intend to hold out that I am an innocent man. But what I did was done for the benefit of the party interested, and not, I solemnly declare, from any idea of fraud—never did such a thought enter my mind : had I been clear of this charge I would never have acknowledged the debt, or paid any thing towards it. All that I ever received was £18 6s. (and not £32, which has been erroneously stated). I paid, at different times, £5, in part of the £18 6s. and for the remainder £13 6s. not being competent to pay it when asked for, I am to suffer death.— I must, in duty to God and the public, declare, that part of the evidence against me from Keswick was false, and has since been detected as such. This materially injured me during my trial ; however, I freely forgive all my prosecutors, perjured witnesses, and others that appeared against me on that fatal occasion.—During the remaining few hours I have yet to live, I shall offer up my prayers for them, and trust they will pray for themselves, as they must very soon follow me into eternity, if not by the hands of the executioner,—the hand of Providence will not exempt them.—May we all, in the language and spirit of Christian forgiveness, meet together in heaven.

" I remain, my dear Sir, your afflicted and affectionate Friend, on the verge of death,

" Cell, Friday, April 23, 1819. " J. TOWNSHEND.

EXECUTION.

On the fatal morning, April 24, the Apparatus of Execution was erected near the Court-Houses, Carlisle. Notwithstanding the near approach of Eternity, Gale maintained his usual stupid insensibility : his fellow-sufferer, on the contrary, was fervent in his devotions, and expressed pleasure, rather than apprehension, at the prospects of quitting this life, saying, " he was quite happy—the happiest man in the world !"—At about a quarter before three o'clock they ascended the platform, with great firmness, and, after joining in prayer with the different ministers who attended them, about ten minutes, they were launched into eternity.

Jollie, Typ.

Execution notice affording full details about Gale and Townshend. Carlisle Library

respectable parents with a brother who had succumbed to a nervous breakdown following his sibling's disgrace. Gale was less responsive, a duller, more irrational individual, but the ministers persevered.

Despite all this, the physical and personal well being of the twosome remained totally neglected and no one appeared greatly concerned to do much about it. The two condemned men were kept in a damp cell without heating. They had neither chair nor stool and only straw to sleep on. Daily they were exposed to the scrutiny of morbid visitors, believed to have paid gaol staff to gain admittance.

But their ordeal would soon be over. The petitions having been unsuccessful, Townshend wrote a moving letter duly published in the *Carlisle Journal*, not denying his guilt but reiterating that false evidence had been laid against him, yet stressing too that he forgave all those who had taken a hand in condemning him. The following morning, on 24 April, the two prisoners heard the gallows being erected close to their place of confinement. Shortly before 3 pm on that day they were led out together before the usual dense crowd, which was much more subdued in this instance. Following ten minutes of prayer they were dispatched into eternity.

By and large it remained an emotive affair, meriting a critical write-up in the local press shortly afterwards; an unusual state of play following most Carlisle executions. All this and more may have contributed at least a little towards influencing local opinion where it mattered at the time. Gale and Townshend were certainly the last ever to be hanged for such offending in the county, though the original verdict in their case has still of itself to surely remain a doubtful matter.

Chapter 9

Nightmare on Chiswick Street 1873

But given the amount of morphine ... the coroner was dissatisfied.

Dr Alexander McLeod was a surgeon in the Indian Army and had been overseas for many years. When he eventually returned to Britain on leave with his wife and children in 1873, it was unclear why he chose to rent a large house in Chiswick Street, Carlisle, the family knowing no one in the area. It may have been that they simply desired peace and quiet close to the Lake District, in one of the more sedate streets in the city, or that they had no one left in Britain at all. Whatever the reason, their sojourn in Carlisle was not destined to bring them anything but grief.

No sooner were they settled in than the eldest son took ill with typhoid fever. Most of the work of nursing the boy fell upon his mother who for days enjoyed no sleep. Slowly the patient began to recover but around 6.30 pm on 15 October, Anne McLeod became confused and incoherent. Her husband called in Dr Walker, a local GP and in a state of mounting anxiety, gave him a number of particulars. That day he had apparently resorted to giving his wife morphine to induce sleep but with catastrophic result.

By this time Mrs McLeod was in a coma on the hearthrug. A stomach pump was promptly utilized, mustard plasters were applied to the woman's legs, and ammonia put to her nostrils, all to no avail. By this time it was 8 pm and the situation was becoming desperate. A third medical man, Dr McLaren was called in. McLaren administered an injection of atropine. Briefly it appeared that Mrs McLeod was beginning to rally. But by 10 pm she was dead.

Given the circumstances, a post mortem was required. This revealed that death was due to an overdose of morphine. McLeod had made no secret of the fact that on 15 October he had dosed his wife repeatedly with the drug to induce sleep. But given the amount of

Chiswick Street today, barely changed since the McLeod tragedy in 1873. Andrew Richardson

morphine in the dead woman's system, the coroner was dissatisfied. Alexander McLeod was subsequently charged with the manslaughter of his wife and appeared before Mr Justice Denman at Carlisle Assizes on 27 February 1874.

By this time the episode was being spoken of as the Chiswick Street Poisoning Case. The doctor had been granted bail following a brief period in custody but still remained under something of a cloud. His defence was that he had become increasingly concerned over the fact that his wife had been so bereft of sleep. He had therefore gone to a local chemist's shop and purchased morphine, giving her the drug in port wine at half hourly periods from 4 pm to 6.30 pm on the day she died.

But how much of the drug had he given, bearing in mind that a grain had of itself been known to kill, even while those better conditioned to it could take more? McLeod ought to have surely known something of the drug's potential, more so given that it was much more commonplace in the East. It was of course also highly addictive.

As it was, the doctor wasn't even sure how many grains he had bought twenty grains or ten grains? There were three grains left in the bottle produced and if this was deducted from ten, then only seven grains had been given over a two and a half hour period. But the doctor admitted that he hadn't been weighing the amounts; he had only been guessing them. And the chemist's assistant was sure he had sold twenty grains to McLeod.

The whole business was a tragic mess. But as the defence emphasized, much did appear to hinge on an individual's ability to absorb morphine. As it was, the accused man apparently considered that he knew how much his wife could safely take. He had been wrong, but had surely had her best interests at heart.

It was left to Judge Denman to sum up and he was at pains to stress that if a drug was administered without want of skill and with good intention, and merely involved some error of judgement, then the prisoner was not guilty and the jury must acquit him which they proceeded to do, followed by applause from the public gallery.

Alexander McLeod left the court a free man and no more was ever heard of him. But presumably he would have his own private burden of sadness to bear for the remainder of his life.

Chapter 10

The Railway Crossing Murder 1861

... the old lady was found battered brutally to death ...

Some years ago, a journalist suggested that murder was a rare crime in Cumberland; the reason why some of the most mundane murder stories have gone into local lore. This is true to an extent, but there have been some heinous local murders too, none more so than the railway crossing murder at Durranhill in November 1861.

The scene of this crime on the eastern side of Carlisle is no more, obliterated by houses, a huge trading estate and a network of roads. But in 1861, the lonely crossing on the Carlisle-Newcastle railway line with its small keeper's cottage was almost completely isolated; a prime target for any predatory criminal. This was compounded by the fact that the crossing keeper was a seventy-two year old widow, Jane Emmerson, who was likely to be out and about alone from 4 am to 10.30 pm opening and closing the crossing gates.

The fact that she had a daughter and two grandchildren living with her may have served as an additional safeguard. But they weren't always there and were all away visiting relatives in Liverpool when the old lady was found battered brutally to death on the morning of 22 November 1861, lying only a short distance from the crossing gates, with one eye forced back completely into her skull. Beside her lay a bloodstained hedge slasher. The cottage had been broken into and ransacked. Teaspoons, linen, as well as money put by for the victim's funeral couldn't be accounted for. A second murder weapon, a bloodstained pickaxe, was discovered under a bed.

The state of the body indicated that the murder must have taken place the previous evening after the crossing gates had been pulled across the line. But now the gates were pulled back again. Surely the killer must be someone local who knew the routine of the victim, the times of the trains, and when Jane Emmerson had been alone? Whoever it was hadn't been too careful either. The imprint of a shoe

The site of Jane Emmerson's cottage. Andrew Richardson

sole had been left on the cottage door, which had been kicked in. There were other footprints at the scene from the same shoes, the design of the sole forming an unusual pattern. Surely the culprit would be quickly run to earth in the light of this?

Yet several weeks passed and no arrest was made. What the public weren't aware of was that the police, though now feeling that they knew who was responsible, still required the shoes to help clinch their case and obtain a conviction. There had also been other pieces of relevant information to tie up. Meanwhile, not wishing to panic the suspect, they chose to lull him into a sense of false security for the moment, even to the extent of taking the local press into their confidence.

Then shortly before Christmas 1861 they acted, arresting a thirty-two year old engine driver, William Charlton, at his home in Harraby Street, situated ironically enough below the site of the former gallows. Charlton, a married man with three children, protested his innocence from the start but, by this time, the police were more than confident he was the culprit. They were additionally certain when the incriminating shoes were discovered in his home with a number of the studs deliberately removed. But Charlton sealed his fate irrevocably when he rashly proceeded to make a statement accusing his brother-in-law, Tom Robinson, of borrowing the shoes from him shortly before the crime. Unfortunately for him, Robinson had a sound alibi for the 21 and 22 November. He had been miles away at the time and knew nothing of the shoes. Since it was such a blatant tissue of lies and perhaps affords us some additional insight into the level of the killer's psyche, the statement is produced here in full:

On Thursday night, the 21st day of November last, I went home from my work about 5.20 pm. Afterwards I came out, and went into the Reading Room, and went over to the engine sheds. When I came from there, Thomas Robinson, my brother-in-law, was standing at the railway yard gates. We spoke to each other. He asked me if I was going up street. We came up street, and went into Mr David Hall's public house, and had each a pint of ale. We sat there a few minutes, not very long. While in there he asked me to lend him my shoes as the roads were very clarty, and his boots were rather tight. So I lent him my shoes. They are the shoes which the police showed me on Saturday at the Court House. We then came out and I left him at the door. He went down Crown Street. He said he was going to Ivegill. I went down Botchergate. I called in at Mabel Andrew's in Union Street, and had two pints of ale. I then went home and went to bed. Chambers called me up on the following morning (Friday) a few minutes past three o'clock. When I was coming out of the house Thomas Robinson came out of our petty and gave me my shoes back again and I asked him where he had been till this time in the morning. He said, 'I have had a bloody good spree.' I saw him no more till the Saturday night following, at the Earl Grey Inn. *When I gave him my shoes in David Hall's the nails were in the soles, and I did not observe them out until Saturday night, the 23rd November, when I was cleaning them. I have told Thomas Robinson never to come near my house again, as he was such a bad 'un. I wish I had never seen him.*

This is correct. – Wm Charlton.

Charlton, of medium height and unremarkable appearance, came to trial early in 1862. Though he persisted in pleading innocent the evidence against him was now more than sufficient. Aside from the clue of the footprints, which clearly matched his shoe soles, there was his foolish attempt to blame an innocent man, putting him fully in the frame. But as it transpired, he had also known Mrs Emmerson and her way of life well. Not only had he driven his train over Durranhill Crossing regularly, he had also had an allotment near the victim's cottage. He had visited her and won her confidence, no doubt weighing up the cottage interior and its contents in the process and deciding that the place was worth robbing. He had even borrowed the pickaxe for use in his garden and knew where it was kept.

Thereafter, it was generally accepted that he had made his way covertly to the cottage on the evening of 21 November after learning that the victim would be alone. It had been dark and stormy at the time but the cottage didn't lie too far from Harraby Street and there was ample foliage at the scene in which to hide out of the rain, with one or other of the murder weapons. When Jane Emmerson came out to close the crossing gates at 10.30 pm and bring in the gate lamps for the night, it was assumed he had sprung out and attacked her; either then, or when she had returned after attending to her duties and found him attempting to break into the locked cottage. Early the following morning, in order to distort the time of the victim's death, he had crept back and reopened the crossing gates. In this instance however, he had been seen by workmates returning from the scene of the crime to the depot, giving them the lame excuse that he had been away obeying a call of nature in nearby bushes, when in fact there was a perfectly good toilet on site.

But why had he felt the need to commit such an appalling crime at all? He had been in regular work and earning better money than many of his contemporaries. He was a good husband and father and popular enough with his workmates, with harmless interests and a close extended family in Northumberland. What emerged however was that there was a darker side to Willie Charlton.

Several years previously, he had been suspected of thieving from a guard's van but acquitted for want of sufficient proof and reinstated by his reluctant employers. And though well paid by the standards of the times, he appeared hard up to the extent that he was accustomed to buying his beer on tick. He also had yet another child on the way, which would, no doubt, involve him in further financial outlay. Possibly Mrs Emmerson's cottage finally proved a target too tempting to resist, by one who hadn't many scruples to the extent that he had been prepared to smear his own wife's brother. But here we are merely into the realms of assumption.

What Charlton did do was maintain his innocence until the end. By way of mitigation, his counsel pointed out that no bloodstains had been discovered on his clothing, nor any stolen property found about him. But, of course, he had had ample time to clean himself up and dispose of what he had taken. Unfortunately for him, he had still been confident enough, or mean enough, to hold on to his shoes. That, and his irresponsible attempt to blame Robinson, were his biggest mistakes. In the light of this and more, there could only be one verdict.

The Durranhill killer quietly mounted the scaffold on the south wall of Carlisle Gaol the following March before the usual heaving crowd, after admitting that he had had a fair trial and exonerating the unfortunate Robinson, though that was as far as he was prepared to go. He calmly bade the prison chaplain goodbye and within minutes he was dead, the last, and one of the most odious murderers, to be hanged publicly in the county of Cumberland.

Chapter 11

Kings by Night
1813

For years he had been a thorn in the side of the local authorities ...

T owards the end of the Napoleonic Wars the area around Carlisle was plagued by a series of armed raids on lonely houses, striking terror into the hearts of the inhabitants. Battered as Britain was following years of warfare with France and consequent deprivation, there were those all the more determined to survive come what may and not too concerned about who they hurt in the process. This was true of the UK as a whole but Cumberland, with its huge tracts of isolated terrain, lent itself particularly well to such skulduggery, the gangs concerned being, if anything, an offshoot of the highwaymen and footpads still operational in many parts of Britain.

Yet badly organized though the forces of law and order remained at the time, they did still have their successes. Hence on 13 September 1813 there appeared before Mr Justice Chambre at Carlisle, thirty year old Daniel McCrory and three of his gang of ruffians, McMahon, Docherty and Gatty, charged with having entered the isolated home of Jonathan Furness in the parish of Torpenhow, with five others, and of robbing it of plate, cash and other articles.

This was putting the facts mildly. The armed gang had descended on the house the previous February, late in the evening, held up the terrified occupants, locked them in a lumber room begging for their lives, then virtually cleared the place of anything at all of value after drinking all the liquor they could find. On this occasion, however, they had erred. McCrory for one had worn no mask and was now clearly identified by a female member of the household. For years he had been a thorn in the side of the local authorities but had somehow succeeded in remaining at large. But in this instance he had been pursued and arrested at Hawick. Furthermore, in addition to the

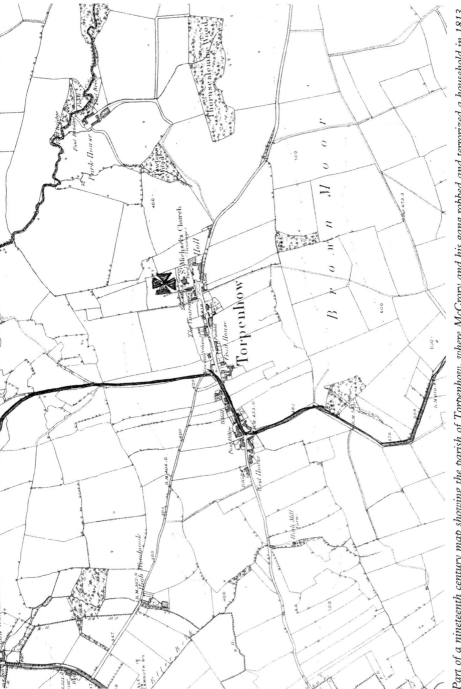

Part of a nineteenth century map showing the parish of Torpenhow, where McCrory and his gang robbed and terrorized a household in 1813.
Carlisle Library

Torpenhow witness, a former gang member, Patrick Gavin, already charged with highway robberies in southern Scotland, had turned King's Evidence to save his skin.

Gavin confirmed what the previous witness had said. He went on to describe how the raid had been planned beforehand at a house in Caldewgate, the home of one Edward O'Neil, whose son had previously lodged in the home of the prospective victims, and of his own participation. Thereafter the verdict was a foregone conclusion. McCrory had already pleaded guilty and while the lives of his associates were spared, he was sentenced to death.

The man himself made an interesting study. He was described at the time as no more than five feet seven inches tall but robust and well made, with a fair complexion and sparkling intelligent eyes, *denoting one determined to command, like Milton's fallen angel*, though he was merely of humble Irish parentage. He was also a competent horseman. Throughout the trial he manifested total indifference, only rousing himself to spit in Gavin's face. Then upon receiving his sentence he bowed respectfully to the jury before being removed.

His execution on 18 September in the region of the old Carlisle Gaol was not dissimilar to that of Dick Turpin at York seventy-four years previously, with a vast crowd kept in order by a picked body of constables and a troop of Dragoon Guards. It was hoped by the authorities that the renegade Irishman, who was suspected of a whole spate of other local robberies, might now make a full confession. He appeared at 3.30 pm, immaculately dressed in black coat, breeches and white stockings. Though previously indifferent to religious approaches he was now accompanied by a Roman Catholic priest.

Only too well aware that this was his moment, he ascended the ladder to the scaffold with a spring in his step. Turning to face the crowd he drew out a sheet of paper and proceeded to deny his involvement in crimes which had been committed in the neighbourhood over the past eighteen months, only admitting to the Torpenhow raid while forgiving his prosecutors. That admission was all the authorities were to get from Danny McCrory.

Even now they were to be embarrassed. The rope was placed around the prisoner's neck and the trap sprung. But the rope snapped and he was thrown to the ground below. It quickly became apparent that his leg was broken. But he didn't cry out, merely reminding the hangman that he had tested the rope beforehand and advised then that it would never hang a man of his weight!

Another rope being found, the condemned man was hoisted back onto the scaffold in a chair and turned off again. The new rope partly gave way and for a moment it was feared the Irishman might come down and break his other leg. But somehow the rope held and, in this instance, death came quickly.

That same evening McCrory was interred in St Cuthbert's churchyard, with a huge concourse of both Cumbrians and Irish in attendance.

Chapter 12

Death at the *Pack Horse Inn* 1861

... he appeared unable or unwilling to resist her attentions.

illiam Horsley was an apprentice draper at Penrith and only nineteen years old when he married Mary Ann Davidson. His parents were people who set a lot of store by respectability. Their son, though well brought up, tended to be weak and indecisive but not without good intentions. Unfortunately, he was to be tested sorely by his mother-in-law, Jane, for it quickly became apparent that she was intent upon competing with her daughter for the young man's affections.

At that time Jane Davidson was landlady of the *King of Prussia*, one of Penrith's many hostelries. A native of Scaleby village and now forty-eight years old, she was still an attractive woman who enjoyed the company of younger men. Some might have found it difficult to believe that she had borne twelve children given that she was so robust and outgoing. There was a husband, George, but the marriage had gone stale and he had become a secondary figure.

Horsley appears to have fallen under his mother-in-law's sway. It was not long before Mary Ann was complaining that he was spending far too much time with her mother. In desperation the young wife appealed to her mother-in-law, who remonstrated with her son. But even though the newly-weds had a home of their own, the older woman continued to monopolize Horsley and he appeared unable or unwilling to resist her attentions.

When Mary Ann fell pregnant, there were those who hoped that this might finally end the unhealthy liaison. But the child only lived a short time. A few months later its mother also died. Penrith being a much smaller place than Carlisle little was confidential and the relationship between Horsley and his mother-in-law had become a source of constant gossip. When Mary Ann died, there were some nasty insinuations. These were groundless. The young wife had died of consumption and her husband did appear genuinely grieved.

Penrith, parts of it scarcely altered at all, where William Horsley and Jane Davidson first met. Andrew Richardson

Mrs Davidson rapidly took on the role of comforter to the bereaved husband. This was all well and good until the widower's mother caught them in a compromising situation. Disgusted, she virtually gave up speaking to Jane Davidson following this.

It was perhaps due to this embarrassing episode that Horsley finally began to see the fool he was making of himself. He was now a fully-fledged draper with no ties and there was no longer anything to detain him in Penrith. Finally he was prevailed upon to move to Carlisle, which appeared far enough away from the infatuated older woman. He found work with a shopkeeper, a Mr Hyslop, and took lodgings in his employer's house.

Mrs Davidson wasn't prepared to let him go so easily. She bombarded him with letters and romantic verses, being no mean hand with a pen. Soon Horsley was travelling back to Penrith to see the older woman in his free time, still unable to free himself. This was not sufficient for Jane. She had to be nearer her young man. Early in 1861 she became landlady of the *Pack Horse Inn* behind Carlisle Railway Station, taking up residence there with her remaining children and extending an invitation to the young draper to visit at any time. By now she and her husband were all but estranged. George Davidson was working out in the country and only returned occasionally, so Horsley had no opposition. He visited the *Pack Horse* regularly and slept there a number of times though there is no evidence that he was actually sleeping with his mother-in-law on these occasions.

Now it was the pious Hyslop's turn to take the younger man aside and lecture him, for tongues were beginning to wag locally as they had done in Penrith. He banned Mrs Davidson from his shop and even threatened to sack Horsley if he didn't take himself in hand. This may have jolted the latter to an extent; soon in fact he began seeing another woman.

Hearing this, Mrs Davidson was distraught and said she would be the end of him. She desperately consulted a fortune-teller, purchasing a number of worthless charms and setting someone to watch Horsley. She then attempted to come between the couple, though how serious their affair was is still open to conjecture.

The fact remained that William Horsley now scarcely knew which way to turn. Finally he made clear that he intended to go to the *Pack Horse* and end things with Jane Davidson once and for all. There she invited him into the front kitchen and they sat closeted together for hours, drinking steadily. No voices were raised in anger and it seemed that the older woman might have won him round again. It was not until nearly midnight than an older daughter, Margaret, heard her mother come upstairs, leaving Horsley in the kitchen. Jane was heard rummaging around and later being sick but finally silence reigned.

It was the following morning before Horsley was discovered on the kitchen floor. His head was resting on a pillow and he had been covered with an eiderdown. At first it was thought he was asleep but upon being uncovered it was obvious he was dead, lying in a pool of blood, his necktie drawn tightly around his throat. He had been strangled with such force that blood had burst from his nose and mouth.

As the public house began to fill up with authority figures, Mrs Davidson was discovered in another room gasping for breath. Soon she too was dead, a post mortem presently revealing a huge amount of arsenic in her stomach.

What had happened that night in the kitchen could only be assumed but it appeared fairly certain that Horsley had been plied with drink by Jane Davidson and then strangled. Whether or not he had gone through with his avowed intention to finally break with her beforehand was uncertain, but she had taken the initiative in any case. Then obviously with no desire to continue without him she had killed herself with arsenic, purchased and secreted earlier.

The verdict at the subsequent inquest was wilful murder of William Horsley against Jane Davidson and self-murder against the same Jane Davidson. It was a sad ending to a sad affair.

66

Chapter 13

The Croglin Vampire
1680–90

Her two brothers ... found her lying with blood seeping from bites on her throat.

When vampires are mentioned nowadays most of us tend to think of Bram Stoker's *Dracula*. This work of horror fiction is drawn primarily from the life and atrocities of the fifteenth century Wallachian warrior, Vlad Draca, and the dark deeds of the Hungarian Countess Elizabeth Bathory (1560–1614), with a generous dash of folklore tradition mixed in. It is not particularly well written but has continued to ensure an ongoing interest in vampirism, thanks also to a whole series of films made from the book.

The vampire tradition in Europe however, pre-dates the Christian era itself, tending to have affected the lives of many unfortunate people before Stoker's novel was ever published in 1897. Nor was it the first Victorian horror story of its kind though it remains by far the most popular.

Given many people's continuing preoccupation with horror and the macabre, it is therefore probably not too surprising that the story of Cumberland's vampire, though on a much lesser scale, remains, in its way, very much part of the county's folklore. It had been with us long before 1897 even while most locals tend to dismiss it lightly. Interestingly enough it does have about it some semblance of authenticity, though it is difficult to date precisely and may have been embellished over the years.

The story familiar to most locals is of a young woman, Amelia Cranswell who, with her two brothers, rented Croglin Grange in the lonely rugged fell country to the east of Carlisle and Penrith. No sooner were they in residence than Amelia received a terrible shock. She had retired to bed in a room on the ground floor when she saw a creature staring at her through the window with piercing eyes. Traumatized, she lay there while the terrifying figure broke a leaded pane, stuck a shrivelled arm inside and pulled down the catch.

Seconds later the intruder was inside the bedroom and bending over her. Emerging from her trauma she began to scream.

Her two brothers broke into the bedroom and found her lying with blood seeping from bites on her throat. The creature, whatever it had been, escaped outside. One of the brothers chased after it but it was too swift for him and disappeared into a churchyard close by. The brother rejoined the others. By this time Amelia was coming round though she remained in a considerable state of shock. Their first thought was that a lunatic had escaped but there was no asylum within miles and no such escape had been reported. It seemed important to leave the area and the brothers took their sister to Switzerland to allow her to recuperate.

There Amelia made a good recovery and was insistent that they all return to Croglin Grange, emphasizing that lunatics didn't escape every day and reminding her siblings that they had taken a lease on the house for a full seven years. The brothers agreed but planned ahead. Their sister would sleep in the same room but with the door unlocked. They would remain close by with pistols at the ready. They didn't have long to wait. Within months of their return the creature appeared again in the same manner but this time the brothers were on the spot before it could climb through the window. As it sprinted off one of them took aim and hit it in the leg. This slowed it down and it was seen climbing laboriously into the churchyard and entering a vault.

Croglin Church. Andrew Richardson

The following day the brothers headed a party of locals and entered the vault. They found the place wrecked. Coffins and their contents were scattered everywhere with one exception which contained the body of a gaunt figure of a man dressed in ancient clothing with blood dripping from his mouth and a bullet in his thigh. No time was wasted; a stake was driven into the creature's heart and its body burnt. There, to all intents and purposes, the story ends.

This is all well and good but there is a lack of tangible information. In a colourful piece written for the *Carlisle Journal* in January 1964, Wilmot Rogers dates the event as taking place towards the latter end of the nineteenth century and describes it as occurring at the present dwelling on the site, Croglin Hall. Some backing for this comes from Valentine Dyall, who gives the date as around 1875. Augustus Hare, writing towards the end of the nineteenth century, mentions Croglin Grange and a tomb. Charles G Harper writing in 1924 said neither of the latter existed.

None of this was very useful. It was the writer F Clive-Ross who probably succeeded in throwing more useful light on the matter, just prior to the Wilmot Rogers article. He visited the remote Croglin area for himself and spoke with a number of locals. He learnt that there had indeed been a Croglin Grange but it had changed its name about 1720 to Croglin Low Hall, otherwise known as Croglin Hall, when it had also been renovated. There had been an older church there too. This had been despoiled by Cromwell's troops under Ireton years before and fallen into ruin along with a burial vault serving the Fisher family, who had lived in Croglin Grange.

The Fishers had eventually removed to Guildford and let the place to people named Cranswell. The stones from the old church had been utilized for the outbuildings of Croglin Low Hall. The current church about two miles away had only been built in 1878 so could have no part in the saga. The episode was felt to have occurred some time between 1680 and 1690 when the original church, or chapel, had fallen into complete ruin but some foundations remained. This appeared more authentic.

Did the episode occur at all? Something untoward may well have taken place given that the story has survived for so long, though whether or not the assailant was anything more than a local oddity has to be a prime consideration. At least it does make a good story.

Chapter 14

A Feast of Poison 1845

There had been a rumour of an improper relationship...

t all began with a head cold refusing to go away. But worse lay in store for forty-five year old Peggy Graham of Kirkandrews village, a few miles west of Carlisle. In late November 1844 after some three weeks, she finally began to improve, only to be suddenly racked by terrible chest pains, vomiting and thirst. On Tuesday evening, 26 November, after being fed a dish of sago by her husband, John, she was worse than ever. The next morning, following renewed medical intervention, there was a slight improvement. This was of short duration; the invalid grew rapidly worse. Her sight and hearing became impaired. She fell in and out of sleep. At 7 pm on the evening of 27 November 1844 she died, and was buried in the local churchyard.

At the time, there were those in the know who had their suspicions, wondering if Peggy Graham had met with foul play. For, contrary to what most continued to think, those closer to home knew all had not been well within the Graham household. John and Peggy Graham had been married fourteen years. At the onset it was seen as a good match. Both were local people. He was the eldest in a family of two boys and two girls. His father, John Graham senior, a yeoman farmer at nearby Grinsdale was universally respected, being both hard working and thrifty as were Peggy's family. John Graham junior went on to rent a farm from his father at neighbouring Kirkandrews and became renowned as one of the best cattle breeders in the district. His doting wife assisted him uncomplainingly. Perhaps unfortunately there were no children, but the couple didn't appear to dwell on this.

More recently however, John Graham had begun to change. A large not unhandsome individual of forty-three years with red whiskers and a pleasant manner, his wife was to describe him as having become unsettled, and accuse him of never having time for her company. There had been a rumour of an improper relationship on his part

Grinsdale village, scene of the second Graham poisoning. Andrew Richardson

with one of the female servants, Margaret Rickerby, the latter having became familiar and insulting towards her mistress, now a delicate nervous woman, who had lost part of the roof of her mouth and was, at times, difficult to understand.

For the moment however, none of this was common knowledge and any rumours died down. It was noted nevertheless that with his wife now in the churchyard and no children to bind him, John Graham had become more unsettled than ever. In vain did his father prevail upon him to continue farming at Kirkandrews. He was resolved to give his tenancy up and did so at the beginning of February 1845. It must all have been very disappointing to John senior that his son and heir had taken such a course, with nothing tangible to put in the place of the occupation at which he had previously excelled, only keeping on a few cows as a passing interest.

In fact the defunct farmer didn't leave Kirkandrews, staying on in his former farmhouse as a lodger of the new bachelor tenant, John Beswick. Otherwise he was still to be seen at the cattle markets and in local hostelries. He didn't appear too well off but continued to be popular with the majority. On other occasions he would drop in on his younger brother, Sibson, married with a family, who also farmed in the area. He maintained contact with his two married sisters and became a more regular visitor to his elderly parents than in the past.

It was at the home of the latter that there occurred the first of the events bringing poison into the equation. The widower had only recently given up his farm and had been visiting his parents some short time afterwards. Like most farming families, the Grahams believed in good sustaining food and parents and son dined off potato pot. Shortly afterwards all three became violently ill, more so the errant son. It was some days before they recovered. Afterwards John junior made a point of approaching a Carlisle druggist, Richard Martindale, whom he knew, and asked him if he could undertake an analysis of the potato pot for arsenic. But it then transpired that the remains of the offending food had been buried in the farm midden. So nothing came of this request, somewhat untoward of itself.

Not a great deal happened for some weeks following this event. But then on Thursday, 15 May, John Graham arrived unexpectedly at his parents' home. He had called to invite his mother, Ruth, to take a trip to Newcastle with him with some talk of visiting old friends and looking at cattle. But this was all too sudden for old Mrs Graham. She was busy in any case baking girdle cakes. The dough had already been prepared and stood in a covered pot in the kitchen. She declined her son's offer. He remained talking with her for an hour before departing alone for Newcastle. No one saw him go near the dough but he had been within reach of it.

At Carlisle he boarded the Newcastle train with his carpetbag, meeting up with some old friends. He never mentioned cattle but spoke of moving to London. In Newcastle he visited no one, spending most of his time at an inn kept by an acquaintance. Then late on Saturday, 17 May 1845, he arrived by train from Newcastle at the *Crown Inn*, Haltwhistle. The landlady, Sarah Saul, recalled him from 8 May when he had been at the *Crown* with a younger woman she was later to identify as Margaret Rickerby. On that occasion he and his companion had had breakfast and remained in excess of three hours in a room upstairs.

In this instance Graham appeared listless and remained until the following Monday, waiting for someone to arrive by train from Carlisle. No one came but what did finally arrive was a message to say his father was dying. He immediately purchased a ticket for Carlisle, remarking what an uncertain thing life was and that his father had been quite well when he left. Even then he didn't visit his seventy-six year old parent immediately but did see him shortly before he died on Tuesday, 20 May 1845, being then in an inebriated state.

On this occasion, so rapid had been the decline of John senior that a post mortem was undertaken. It was quickly established that death had been as a result of arsenic poisoning, with the conclusion that this had been in the girdle cakes, given that several other people had suffered varying degrees of sickness after eating them. In John senior's case the result had been fatal, the old man having already been in failing health and more vulnerable.

Following a preliminary inquest and some concerned discussion, it was now but a short step to making application for the exhumation of Peggy Graham. Her widowed husband was distraught, saying he would rather be shot than that she should be lifted but he no longer had any say in the matter. On 6 June 1845 the body was exhumed and laid out in a barn. Following the formality of identification by the dead woman's brother, the pathologists went to work, discovering arsenic in the corpse's stomach, gullet and bowels. Shortly afterwards John Graham was arrested, lying in bed at Beswick's farm in the same room where his wife had died six months previously. He was charged with poisoning his wife and father and lodged in Carlisle Gaol.

The inquest on Peggy Graham was one of the longest and most intense in Cumberland's history. John Graham junior may have enjoyed some standing in the community but the authorities were determined to get to the bottom of the matter and went about the business relentlessly, sparing no one's feelings. The inquest as a whole went on for several days and, in the process, everything unsavoury about the former farmer was laid bare, with a stream of witnesses testifying for or against him.

One of the most damning was Graham's former manservant, Ben Mitchell, who remained doggedly supportive of the dead woman. He spoke of the improper relationship between Graham and the coarse, ill-educated Margaret Rickerby, which had eventually resulted in his mistress being on the receiving end of a stream of verbal insolence from the girl. Yet John Graham had it seemed, rarely attempted to intervene. After Peggy Graham's death, Mitchell claimed to have seen the widower and Rickerby going off together from the Carlisle hiring fair. On a more ominous note, he spoke of having discovered a parcel of rat poison in the turnip house at Kirkandrews shortly before John senior's death. He had given it to Beswick who, it transpired, had had it destroyed. But here was evidence that there had been poison on the premises

Another hostile witness was the dead woman's brother, Joseph Hind, who hadn't liked Graham's churlish attitude during Peggy's final days, to the extent that he hadn't spoken to him since. Others spoke of the husband wanting to do everything himself in the sick room, even chasing away his own mother and sister. Neither had he apparently hurried to bring the doctor back when it was felt the latter was needed. Special emphasis was placed on the fact that his wife had been worse after he had fed her the sago pudding on the Tuesday prior to her death.

The scene switched back to Graham's relationships with his female servants. Shortly before his wife's death, he had brought one Liz

Graham to Carlisle for some ambiguous discussion. It transpired that she had been pregnant. It was also said he had bought her a bottle of rum. When asked if she had been in the family way to Graham, she had denied this emphatically. But it must have been pondered as to why a master was going out of his way to such an extent on behalf of a female servant, when his wife had more need of him at the time.

Upon Margaret Rickerby being called, at first she was brazen and evasive. She said she had been Graham's servant for almost four years, until November last, but wouldn't say why she had left his service, merely saying she didn't intend to hire again. She admitted that she had been in Saul's pub at Haltwhistle with Graham and that they had also been together all night in another pub, the Grapes, but denied sleeping with him there. She claimed to have been chasing after wages owed to her. But somehow she never appeared too convincing, even when threatened with transportation for perjury.

On the other hand, Martindale, the Carlisle druggist, was emphatic that never in his recollection had he sold John Graham any poison. A fellow druggist, John Sibbald, said likewise. William Reeves, a surgeon, denied that Graham had ever asked him to procure an abortion for Liz Graham. And hadn't Graham been ill himself from poisoning earlier in the year?

Paradoxically, ensconced in Carlisle Gaol, the prisoner was implying that he knew who had administered the poison but that he would keep it to himself!

The jury were not to be sidetracked in any way. At the end of it all, their verdict was succinct and to the point:

That Margaret Graham died from arsenic.
That such arsenic was administered by design.
That the person who administered it was John Graham.

This still left the adjourned inquest on John Graham senior to be taken up. Here Sarah Saul was a key witness, confirming the prisoner's erratic behaviour while staying at her inn in Haltwhistle, waiting for someone from the west who never came. His mother then spoke of events surrounding the baking of the girdle cakes and of her late husband having recently made some payments on her eldest son's behalf. Clearly John Graham junior was far from solvent but his mother refused to criticize him.

The coroner still remained concerned to establish whether or not Graham had purchased any poison at all. With the poison discovered by Mitchell destroyed, and Martindale and Sibbald denying having sold anything of the kind to the prisoner, a druggist from Newcastle was produced, Walker Swan, who thought he might have supplied a man answering the description of Graham with arsenic the previous year; but neither he nor his son could be absolutely positive. It was only left for a medical witness, Thomas Elliot to confirm that arsenic had been discovered in a surviving girdle cake.

In essence, the coroner felt that there was a lot which remained inconclusive. There had been two deaths in the same family but there were still doubts about the old man's death. Was Mrs Graham guilty? She had baked the cakes after all. But this was doubtful; she had been affected twice by poison herself. Yet her eldest son had been affected too, earlier in the year. Neither had the latter apparently had the opportunity of seeing the dough in the pot on the fatal day. Yet what had been John Graham's object in visiting then at such short notice? How could he have expected his mother to be ready? True, he had still gone to Newcastle, claiming to be looking for a place to keep cows. Had it been his original design however, to get his mother clear of the fate he had planned for his father for in Newcastle he visited no one. He had gone on to behave strangely at Haltwhistle, and then when he did see his father afterwards, was intoxicated. Did he purchase poison in Newcastle? Who else in the family might have committed the crime? Sibson Graham had certainly disposed of the potato pot quickly, eliminating any chance of analysis. A cake had also been destroyed on his wife's orders. The dung heap containing the evidence had been removed on the day before his father's inquest. This did not mean that Sibson was guilty of course, only that his conduct had made the enquiry the more difficult.

All this was pertinent enough and the jury heard him out before returning fairly quickly with their second verdict:

That the deceased John Graham died from the effect of poison wilfully administered to him and that they recorded a verdict of Wilful Murder against some person or persons unknown.

This still left the Kirkandrews farmer to face trial for the murder of his wife. The trial was set for Wednesday, 6 August 1845. It emerged that he would be very much in the hands of his own kind for most of the jury were farmers.

In fact there were to be two trials as matters evolved, it being presently decided to try Graham for the murder of his father as well. Neither would continue as long as the inquest. Most of the proceedings were a rehash of the former, with many of the original witnesses being recalled and not saying much which was new, the prisoner seated with a handkerchief permanently to his face.

At the onset, Ben Mitchell afforded the court additional snippets, advising that his master had often been missing from home late in the evening at the same time as Margaret Rickerby. The manservant also spoke of Graham having taken to visiting a house in the village with a bad reputation. This did not prove a great deal however and the two Swans could still not positively identify the prisoner as the man who had purchased arsenic at their shop in 1844, even while they did appear more certain in this instance.

More thought-provoking evidence came from Superintendent Sabbage, who had recently emptied the pockets of a coat, waistcoat and trousers belonging to the accused. The clothes had been hanging in his bedroom at Kirkandrews. Mixed amongst breadcrumbs, cheese and woolly matter were traces of arsenic. Could the trap be closing on John Graham again?

This did not appear to be the view of the defence counsel, Wilkin, as he airily began to address the jury, continuing to do so for almost two hours. His salient points were that there was no proof of any improper intimacy between his client and Margaret Rickerby, and hadn't he got rid of her last November in any case? There had only been one instance of reproach from the lips of his wife. He pooh-poohed the evidence of Mitchell and others and contended that everything pointed to John Graham having been a kind husband. And given that Sewell the doctor had prescribed a powder which came from a druggist in the lowest part of Carlisle, mightn't arsenic have been accidentally substituted for the rhubarb and magnesia?

To some it may have appeared that he was skating on thin ice but he carried on, now playing what he probably saw as his trump card. This was the revelation that there was a very strong reason as to why John Graham should wish his wife to live. Years before he had borrowed £200 from his in-laws. If there were no children, in the event of his wife's death, it had been decreed that this sum must be repaid, which it had been. He called upon the jury to acquit his client, before proceeding to call three character witnesses. The first was James Steel, Mayor of Carlisle, the second a clergyman, the third the attorney for the prosecution no less! All spoke well of Graham.

Judge Baron Rolfe's summing up was long and detailed but what he said in sum was that there was no doubt Mrs Graham had died of arsenic, but who had given the poison? John Graham must have had many opportunities, but others in the house had had the same opportunities. And had John Graham the motive? Personally, he had discovered very little motive. There was Rickerby but she had been discharged the previous year and there was no evidence of any illicit

James Steel, Mayor of Carlisle 1845–46, who gave evidence in support of John Graham. Andrew Richardson

intercourse. There was also the factor of the £200 agreement to consider.

The judge droned on. Certainly Graham had had the opportunity but was the motive satisfactory? As for buying poison, the Swans weren't certain of their customer's identity. There was the arsenic in the pockets of the prisoner's clothing of course. But if he had had it in June, had he had it in November 1844? No arsenic had been found in the clothes he was wearing at the time of his arrest. If there had been, this would have proved he had arsenic in his possession. As it was, the other clothes had not been examined until two weeks later, when they would have been accessible to other people. And if John Graham was guilty, he must have been reckless indeed not to conceal the poison better.

Perhaps surprisingly, the judge made no real attempt to divine the prisoner's comment about knowing who had poisoned his wife. Nor did he attempt to make anything of Graham's repeated query at the time of his arrest as to whether or not the police had been to Newcastle to make enquiries? He had other things to say but all in all, appeared favourably disposed towards the prisoner. The result was a finding of not guilty at 8.45 pm, following but one day's trial. The outcome may well have caused some surprise to many of those both packed into the courtroom and thronging the street outside.

Two days later, Graham was tried for the murder of his father. This was an even lesser affair throwing up nothing new. There was fresh play on the prisoner's surprise visit to his mother on 15 May, but still nothing to suggest that he had known she was baking or that he had put anything in the dough. Wilkin for his part was soon in full cry again, admitting that Graham had behaved erratically at Haltwhistle but was this sufficient to condemn him? It was true that he had been in default of a debt prior to this but his father had paid this for him. It was further emphasized that though Graham senior had recently made his will, no one knew the contents of this excepting Mrs Graham. And hadn't the prisoner been poisoned himself earlier in the year? Then the Swans were called yet again but could add nothing.

The wily defence counsel made especial play on the fact that there was even less evidence of opportunity to mix poison in this instance than there had been before. Referring yet again to the discovery of the arsenic in the pockets, he was at special pains to enquire if it were possible that a man who was capable of designedly obtaining poison with the intention of deliberately poisoning his parent, could consider himself secure after leaving the residue of the poison in his clothing and taking off for Newcastle?

The judge appeared to agree with much of this, recapitulating the fact to the jury and, in doing so, appearing to express his view of the case to be that it was not one upon which the jury could satisfactorily believe without doubt, that the crime alleged had been committed. Following this, the result was almost a foregone conclusion. After a mere fifteen minutes, a verdict of not guilty was returned. John Graham was again a free man and promptly vanished from the area.

This was the end, akin to an almost feeble whimper, to one of the most puzzling and intensively reported criminal cases in Cumberland. All these years later, we are still left with the tantalizing question that if Graham didn't poison his wife and father with arsenic, who did? No further attempt ever appears to have been made to find out, with a whole raft of other questions either brushed over or left unanswered.

For instance, why was no effort made at all to confirm whether or not the packet of poison discovered in the turnip house by Mitchell had been tampered with originally? Who was John Graham waiting for so anxiously at Haltwhistle? Could it have been Margaret Rickerby, with whom he appears to have been besotted and who might have known more than she ever revealed? What did the accused man really mean when he indicated that he knew who had administered the poison? Why was he so anxious to know if the police had been to Newcastle to make enquiries prior to his arrest? And why did it take the police so long to collect his spare clothes from Kirkandrews and check them over?

Unfortunately, we shall never really know.

Chapter 15

A Shot in the Head
1820

... he was discovered dead in a gutter on the plantation, shot through the head ...

Most of those we have already encountered here did at least confess to their crimes. James Lightfoot never did and there were some in his day who believed in him. Yet there does seem little doubt that he was guilty of the squalid crime for which he was tried, even while he was found guilty on purely circumstantial evidence.

Cumberland, like many other parts of Britain in 1820, was in a troubled social and economic state following the Napoleonic Wars. James Lightfoot had been as badly served as many; a working class lad from Wigton, one of nineteen children, illiterate, unskilled and poor, his mother widowed. To compound his problems he had had to get married at the age of eighteen after his girlfriend became pregnant.

But then opportunity knocked with the offer of a job at Scarrow Hill Farm in the parish of Cumwhitton, a few miles east of Carlisle. Within weeks the burly teenager appeared well settled with his master, John Leech. He had also formed a close friendship with a local tailor's son, Thomas Maxwell, a youth not much older than himself. The pair spent time regularly in one another's company when not at work. Lightfoot became almost like one of Thomas's family.

The Maxwells were probably slightly better off than the majority of their neighbours. The father made clothes for the locals. His son, Thomas, was also a tailor, and travelled regularly about the countryside collecting money due from farm servants and others.

Such was the state of play when early on Friday, 19 May 1820, Tom Maxwell's sister, Ann, was hailed by Lightfoot from a field where he was ploughing. He asked her what time her brother would be coming home and whether he had any money on him? In all innocence, the girl said it would be night when her brother got home and that she thought he had some money. Some time later she saw

Parish of Cumwhitton today, not greatly changed since the brutal Lightfoot shooting in 1820. Andrew Richardson

Thomas off with eleven shillings in his purse. This was the last she ever saw of him.

From his home at Marthwaite, Maxwell travelled about, finally coming to Scarrow Hill Farm around 2.30 pm. Here he anticipated collecting four shillings from his pal, Lightfoot, who asked Leech for the money. Leech handed over four shillings but Lightfoot wasn't seen to pay Maxwell who went into the farmhouse for a smoke.

Time being money, Leech presently instructed Lightfoot to harrow a nearby field. Complaining of a sprained ankle, Lightfoot refused. Leech's nephew undertook the task instead and Leech went off on other business, leaving Maxwell in the house and Lightfoot in the barn. When the farmer returned around 4 pm. Maxwell was gone but he saw Lightfoot about fifteen minutes later return with a gun, which was normally kept in the house for shooting game.

Around 8 pm, master and man went out on respective trips, to Holme Wrangle and Hornsby. About 10 pm, Leech saw Lightfoot on the road leading from a plantation which lay close to the farmhouse, but in an opposite direction to Hornsby. Lightfoot said he had been attending to cattle near the plantation.

Meanwhile, Thomas Maxwell had completely vanished. It was not until 26 May that he was discovered dead in a gutter on the plantation, shot through the head, his purse lying empty beside him. It was deduced that he had been shot at close range given the nature of the wound and that death had been instantaneous.

James Lightfoot had already left Leech's employment a trifle abruptly on 20 May with what money was due to him. About the same time, Leech had thought to examine the farm gun, finding it unloaded but foul, as though it had recently been fired. There was also sand sticking to the barrel, sand common only to the plantation.

Following the discovery of the body, all roads appeared to lead to Lightfoot. He was taken into custody by a constable and charged with the crime. The teenager vehemently denied everything. He admitted to having had the gun on 19 May but merely to shoot a cuckoo for his master to dress fishing hooks with. He claimed to have gone to the plantation to do this but the bird had gone. He said he had returned to the barn and fired at a magpie out of one of the air holes; that he had then reposed himself before replacing the gun in its former place in the farmhouse.

This scarcely sounded convincing. The youth was remanded in custody and on 17 August 1820 came to trial at Carlisle. There was ample evidence against him. No one had seen him shoot Maxwell, but both Mrs Leech and her husband had seen him, as he hurried back to the farm from the direction of the plantation on the fatal afternoon with the gun. No one had heard a shot fired from the barn but a local man had heard the report of a gun in the plantation on 19 May about 3.30 pm and had seen Lightfoot coming from that direction. Another witness had also heard the sound of gunfire from the same place.

John Leech's nephew, William, confirmed that he had never fired the gun since March, nor did he know anyone else who had except the accused. John Leech testified that he had never given Lightfoot directions to fire at any bird; he admitted that he was acquainted with fishing, knew the feathers used, but never fished. Most damning of all was the sand on the gun barrel, which could only have came from the plantation.

The trial continued for almost nine hours but it only took the jury an hour and five minutes to find the prisoner guilty. Whereupon he struck the bar before him, saying he was a murdered man. Yet during his trial he had seemed to regard the proceedings with the utmost indifference. With only one full day left before his execution he now devoted the time to dictating a letter, still continuing to maintain his innocence, to his wife, who had borne his child on the day of the murder.

My Dear Wife

I am extremely sorry that I have brought so much grief and shame upon you and my other relations, but I solemnly declare that of the crime of murder, for which I am to suffer the awful sentence of the law, I am as innocent as the child unborn. And I freely from my heart forgive my prosecutors and those who have sworn against me, and I hope God Almighty will also forgive them. And I also hope that my untimely death will never be a reflection upon any of you, either upon my brothers or sisters, as long as you live in this world. I remain, my Dear Wife, your unfortunate husband, 'James Lightfoot'.

A similar letter was sent to his mother who had continued to believe in him. The following day he mounted the scaffold before Carlisle Court Houses and addressed the assembled crowd: 'Good people, I am innocent, I am an innocent man, but I forgive all my prosecutors and all the world.'

Some appeared to believe him and he was almost likeable with his ruddy, open countenance. Others felt they had come to know him for what he really was. The noose went around his neck and death came within a few minutes. Afterwards his body was given to the surgeons.

Chapter 16

Death at Kingstown 1860

The charge was manslaughter through gross negligence ...

harles Dicken's *Martin Chuzzlewit* is not the best novel he wrote but it does contain one especially memorable character. There can be few followers of the novelist who are not acquainted with Mrs Gamp, the slovenly, manipulative, self-styled nurse with a fondness for strong drink. Unfortunately, there were all too many of her kind around in those days, a fact Dickens wished to convey. Despite continuing progress on many fronts, nursing still came a poor second in early Victorian Britain.

It would be wrong to say that Mary McVitie of Kingstown, Carlisle was quite in this category. True, she was totally illiterate, but had somehow made her way as a nurse for many years without controversy. However, at sixty-four years of age, she finally found herself in court at Carlisle in February 1860. The charge was manslaughter through gross negligence and lack of skill in the case of a young expectant mother, Tamar Hartley.

The two women were neighbours. On 18 October 1859 the younger woman, now well advanced in labour, was attended by McVitie, who had been sent for and whom she appeared to trust. But her condition deteriorated. When her husband, a policeman, returned from his duties at the court, a neighbour suggested a doctor be sent for. McVitie would have none of this saying she could cope, which appeared questionable. The husband grew increasingly concerned and eventually a Dr Carlyle became involved.

The birth had been one known as an arm presentation. But McVitie, instead of pulling at the emerging child's arms, had had hold of its head, impeding delivery. In the process, one of its arms had became broken, swollen and injured and the baby died. The doctor made no secret of his opinion of McVitie and her bungling. He turned the child and, after waiting until nature took its course, rode home to nearby Carlisle leaving the older woman by the bedside.

The suburb of Kingstown, Carlisle, in the 1920s. Carlisle Library

At 3.00 am he returned but Mrs Hartley was worse and shortly afterwards she too died. Such an outcome resulted in the inevitable post mortem. The vagina and lower part of the womb were found to be bruised and torn, caused it was said by dragging at the child. The nurse appeared to be the culprit, having implied that she possessed all the necessary skills when she did not, causing death as a result.

In court, Carlyle said he was confident that nothing had happened during his visit to cause such injuries. There had been no symptom when he first visited which could have led him to infer such. The fact that McVitie had earlier been so incapable in effecting the delivery however, led him to the conclusion that she had, in her ignorance, damaged the womb. Loss of blood and shock had done the rest.

It therefore appeared that McVitie, in the execution of her duties, had shown gross ignorance and want of skill and could be facing a prison sentence. But under cross-examination the GP then admitted that a case of a ruptured vagina might occur in an arm presentation without blame being imputable to anyone.

Hearing this, the judge immediately interrupted. How could the case go on then, he enquired, given such an answer? Mary McVitie may have been negligent, she may have been ignorant, but how could it be said that this caused death, when it couldn't be known whether the injuries from which death had resulted were produced by McVitie or by natural causes?

The doctor had no tangible answer to this. Nor had a medical colleague, Elliot, who remarked that the injuries in the vagina and uterus might have taken place and the woman may not have died, even while he inclined to the belief that the rent in the vagina had been caused, not by the passage of the child, but by a misdirected hand and that death was attributable to exhaustion, chiefly from protracted labour and haemorrhage, which he did feel could be attributable to McVitie.

The judge had heard enough. He again interfered and said that as Elliot had stated that the rupture might have occurred without necessarily producing death, he must say that he would be obliged to inform the jury that they could not return a verdict of guilty. The jury agreed, promptly returning a verdict of not guilty and Mary McVitie left the court a free woman.

Once again nineteenth century law had taken its course, but whether or not the public agreed wholeheartedly with the verdict in this instance was probably open to some doubt.

Chapter 17

A Triple Hanging 1820

They ... were the last offenders ... to be hanged for anything less than murder.

Danny McCrory was one of the more colourful criminals to meet his end at Carlisle. Despite his villainy, he obviously engendered a measure of grudging admiration, however misplaced. Such never applied in respect of the three uncouth misfits who found themselves at Carlisle seven years later charged with an offence not dissimilar to that of the mercurial Irishman and his gang, but which resulted in three hangings as opposed to one.

John Little alias John Sowerby aged thirty-eight years, William Armstrong aged twenty-two and John Woof aged forty-eight, were accused of feloniously breaking and entering the dwelling house of John Wilson of Soulby in the Parish of Dacre on the night of 22 December 1819 and taking away cash and cloth. All three pleaded not guilty.

Eamont Bridge in 2005, where the plan to commit the Dacre robbery was formulated. Andrew Richardson)

The offence was almost a repeat performance of that perpetrated by McCrory and his acolytes. The war with the French was now over but times remained hard and villainy persisted. Just prior to the deed, the trio held a planning meeting with another reprobate, Tweedale, at Armstrong's home in Eamont Bridge near Penrith. All were professional criminals and well armed with pistols and swords. Armstrong did most of the talking, knowing of Wilson's home and the conditions prevailing there, having recently lived in the same area.

They proceeded there that same night, donned masks and forced an entry, demanding the £100 they believed to be concealed on the premises. It transpired that the money was in a Penrith bank but they ransacked the house nevertheless, after locking the family and their servants in a room upstairs. They even took a servant's umbrella and sneeringly asked her what she had been doing over the past thirty years to have no more than eight shillings to give them? They demanded bread and cheese and having eaten this, made off with everything they could carry including gin and wine.

Like McCrory and his gang, they were not physically violent at the time. On the other hand, no resistance had been forthcoming from their terrified victims. They returned to Little's house, at Clifton Dikes, where he lived with the wife he had bigamously married. Here they shared out the loot and drank the gin and wine. They then split up and might have got away with the crime altogether. But, as in McCrory's case, one of the gang talked upon being arrested for another offence and was prepared to turn King's Evidence to save his neck. This was Tweedale, a boyhood friend of Armstrong. Soon the other three had been rounded up from as far away as Newcastle-upon-Tyne. Their former partner duly testified against them. Some of the stolen property was also belatedly traced to them, thereby cementing the case.

It took little time to find the trio guilty. There were many other offences the authorities wanted to know about, suspecting that the same gang, originally nine in number, had been active in perpetrating. Little, the leader, was questioned but it is unknown how useful the interview proved to be. He was given little time in any case for the powers-that-be were primarily concerned to follow through quickly on the death sentences, which had been imposed on all three.

These were carried out on a corner of the old Carlisle Gaol on 2 September 1820, on the same scaffold where James Lightfoot had recently been dispatched. None of the trio had responded to religious instruction and had spent most of their final hours exchanging lewd jokes. Armstrong struggled hard when attempts were made to pinion him prior to the hanging. Little, a ferocious sight with his long

A map showing the Parish of Dacre in 1822. Carlisle Library

uncombed black beard threatened to break the hangman's neck and kicked out savagely at him before the blindfold went over his eyes. Woof, a former soldier, adopted a more self-disciplined stance at the end, but it seems the local public, as a whole, were not sorry to see the end of all three.

They are notable in that they were the last offenders in Cumberland to be hanged for anything less than murder.

Chapter 18

Blood on the Rake Shank 1834

... he never expressed any regret for the life of the woman he had taken ...

Events leading to John Pearson's appointment with the hangman began on 13 October 1834 when he and his wife arrived at the *Abbey Bridge Inn*. The building is still there today, lying two miles north of the town of Brampton and close to Lanercost, famous for its priory dating back to 1166. All around there remains an abundance of meadows and woodland, pervaded by an air of peace and tranquillity. Not too far distant lies Naworth Castle. Little has changed over the centuries.

It was doubtful if any of this meant much to Pearson though he had lived in the area for a number of years. Forty-seven years old, short and rotund, garbed in tartan trousers and a moleskin jacket which had seen better days, he had sufficient to do earning his living as a farm

The former Abbey Bridge Inn, *John Pearson's local.* Andrew Richardson

labourer, with intervals between as a drainer and mole catcher. A more lucrative sideline was poaching for which he was well known, having served time in prison for his offending.

The woman with him was his second wife, Jane, a complete contrast, a quiet unassuming personality, only forty-four years old and still attractive with raven black hair. The couple had only been married six weeks, Pearson's previous wife having succumbed to consumption leaving several children, though none remained in contact with their father.

The couple arrived at 6 pm. Pearson may have already been partially inebriated. As it was, he drank steadily on at the inn and would have sat longer had his wife not suggested that he conclude his drinking at home; undoubtedly a grave mistake on her part. Though comfortably ensconced he nevertheless agreed to go but not before he had purchased a gill of rum to take with him, along with a portion of coals given the damp autumn weather.

At around 8 pm the couple left the inn, Jane Pearson dutifully carrying the gill of rum. They set off over the bridge outside and wended their way along the lane to Lanercost before striking off uphill towards their dwelling at an isolated place known as Randylands.

What happened during their journey there remains shrouded in mystery. According to Pearson at his trial, he and his wife had both been drunk and he had lost her along the track. He then met a man with her basket in a field. He retrieved the basket but there was still no sign of Jane and she had the door key. He went to seek her without success. The next thing he remembered was waking up in bed with his wife beaten and bloodied beside him. She had spoken of a man taking advantage of her. He had gone off searching vainly for the man and had returned home to find his wife dead.

There was no more than an element of half-truth in any of this and indeed he was to admit to some culpability later. Certainly he was said to have been the worse for drink at the inn. This could well have been the case but no one was saying his wife was drunk at all. On the other hand, he could easily have staggered away from her in the darkness, his condition made even worse by the cold air outside, while she plodded on up the winding track alone, setting down the basket close to home while waiting for him to catch up but unable to locate it again in the darkness. Others did locate it. The son of a labourer named Hewer found it and the latter returned it to the rotund drunkard shortly afterwards. But following this, Pearson's attempt at a defence didn't add up at all. There were too many witnesses.

There is also some confusion over the time but another Randylands tenant, Rachel Whitehead, heard the couple return together before the evening was too far advanced, shortly before Hewer's son discovered the missing basket. Upon receiving it back Pearson was heard to mumble a few words of thanks, before staggering back to his wife with whom he had already been arguing. The rum was in the basket, which would no doubt have been an added cause for agitation on his part at the thought of losing it. He had already lost the coals.

Their residence itself was no grand establishment; a single storey building, little better than a bothy, served by a well at the front and standing virtually on the bed of the Roman Wall. It was divided into small rooms to accommodate the transient labour force employed in the surrounding woods and on local farms. Given that Rachel Whitehead was there that night it would surely have been no great problem gaining admittance whether or not Pearson had a key. However, she was to reiterate that she heard him and his wife arrive together. Seemingly he chose to make the issue of the key a further excuse as part of his defence.

No sooner were the basket and its contents recovered and the couple inside than we can probably assume Pearson began drinking again and became more inflamed. Certainly it was shortly afterwards that Rachel Whitehead, occupying an adjoining room, heard the man drunkenly accusing his wife of infidelity. Then he began to beat her. She cried 'murder' but still the beating continued. Whitehead had only lived at Randylands a few days and scarcely knew the Pearsons. Her husband was working away and she was too terrified to interfere. The beating continued at intervals until almost midnight but the unfortunate woman never cried out again, suffering it seemed merely because she had misplaced the basket, which had been quickly discovered and handed back by another man.

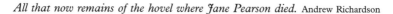

All that now remains of the hovel where Jane Pearson died. Andrew Richardson

At daybreak Pearson left the hovel and retraced his steps in the direction of Lanercost. About 8.30, Jane Pearson cried out to her neighbour, requesting a cup of tea. Whitehead obliged, noting that the other woman was naked and bloody but refusing to speak of her ordeal. Meanwhile, Pearson had arrived back at the inn and brandishing his empty rum bottle, demanded a further pint, appearing tolerably sober again and never mentioning his wife.

It was around 11 am when he again reached Randylands, confronting Rachel Whitehead and beginning to rant about his wife's infidelity, striking out afresh at her before threatening to finish the frightened neighbour. Whitehead ran off and encountered another local woman, Sarah Thirlwell, who went along to the hovel and peered through a window. Pearson, now totally out of control, was wielding a huge rake shank. Thirlwell retreated but shortly afterwards a pedlar, James Barrett, passed the premises and saw Jane Pearson lying naked outside. She staggered back indoors and her husband followed her, mouthing curses.

Barrett raised the alarm and a small crowd converged on Randylands. Jane Pearson could be seen through the window lying on the blood-soaked bed, half covered by a quilt, ominously still. Pearson was swigging from his bottle, telling everyone his wife was dead. Such proved to be true. The rake shank, covered with blood and hair, was found beside her.

Events moved swiftly thereafter. The drunken man was arrested and promptly lodged in Carlisle Gaol. At the onset he was totally disorientated, a prey to delirium tremens, but by the time of his trial in March 1835, had settled down considerably. Needless to say, given the appalling bruises discovered on the victim's body and a huge wound on the back of her head which were believed to have been the ultimate cause of death, there could be only one outcome, with one witness after another testifying against the prisoner. Bloodstained bedding, clothing and the rake shank, five feet long and one and a half inches wide were all produced in court, yet when sentence of death was passed by Baron Parker, everyone appeared moved except Pearson. He simply asked for his hat, clapped it on his head and stepped from the dock, as though totally indifferent to his fate.

Nonetheless, he only had forty-eight hours left to live and called for paper and pens. He wished to produce a statement and desired that it be made public. Perhaps surprisingly, the finished result, though probably edited to some extent, still demonstrates clearer insight and honesty after all, than many might have supposed him to possess. Most of it is reproduced here:

I John Pearson, was born in Cornwood, near Haltwhistle in the County of Northumberland and am now in my 47th year. My father died when I was ten years of age. At the age of thirteen my mind was launched into a world of vanities. I first commenced with my dog and gun and continued in this sporting for upwards of thirty years, for which I often paid dear for my folly by sundry imprisonment and fines, attended with much slavery and often even at the peril of my life. At the age of about eighteen years I fell into an evil habit of drinking which is the mother of many evils and not easy to be shaken off. It creates all kinds of sinful lusts and desires and those that continue in the practice seldom fail to obtain for themselves utter ruin. I often profaned the Lord's Day and neglected the diverse service of God who is the author of all goodness and it is he alone who can sustain us if only we will call upon his name with an earnest desire and serve him faithfully in spirit and in truth. In the course of those thirty years I was four years a gamekeeper in Scotland and better situations no man need wish for, yet could not be content but gave myself up to drinking, and women, and other evil habits, created through the same, until I was dismissed from my service. I at this time had a wife and two children, which I had during the four years neglected. I then enlisted to be a soldier and in about a year, the Captain made me his servant. I remained with him about three years; he then got me my discharge upon my request. Through the help of God I had many comfortable situations in my lifetime and I may say the greatest number of them were lost by excess of drinking. My former wife being dead, leaving five children, I was then left to myself in the world. I came into the parish of Denton, near Brampton, where I wrought for some time. Last I wrought for Mr Thomas Taylor, a family remarkable in both moral and religious duties. I was well used and had constant employment. I had the best advice and example shown me. Being in a state of intoxication (it is like a dream to me) yet I remember of ill-using my wife, but not with the intention to take away her life, although through passion, jealousy and being influenced with drink, I might have inflicted on her the wound that caused her death. I die in peace with all mankind. Signed John Pearson.

With his testament completed, Pearson was only concerned to choose his resting place in the prison yard. Finally it was agreed that he could be buried near the pump. This brutish but not unintelligent individual was hanged in his clogs before a huge crowd on Friday, 13 March 1835. To the end he never expressed any regret for the life of the woman he had taken, but didn't appear too concerned about dying either.

Chapter 19

Grave Robbing in Carlisle 1823

... though the coffin lid had been wrenched off, they were relieved to find the body intact ...

Given the vagaries of the law as it long related to the release of bodies to the medical fraternity for teaching purposes, it scarcely seems surprising that grave robbing flourished for so many years. It was not until the early 1830s that bodies could be obtained legally, those of convicted felons having been the only exceptions until then. Prior to this, most anatomical teachers were heavily dependent upon grave robbers to supply the necessary corpses.

Carlisle and district seem to have been spared the activities of these unfeeling wretches for many years. But in 1823 it appeared that they had finally arrived. In the *Cumberland Pacquet* of 8 December, there is a fulsome half column devoted to the details of bodies being conveyed to the anatomists in Edinburgh from Carlisle.

It began with a rumour that a grave in the Stanwix churchyard had been desecrated. Concerned locals opened the grave and though the coffin lid had been wrenched off, they were relieved to find the body intact, presumably because it had been found to be no longer fresh. But other churchyards in the city had also been desecrated and attention shifted to a local carrier's warehouse where a large wooden crate resembling a coffin had recently arrived.

The carrier, having already received discreet information from Edinburgh that bodies had been received there from the Carlisle area, was at once on his guard. However, two men almost immediately called and took the box away. Seen later in the vicinity by suspicious locals, they were asked what had become of the box? They responded frankly, saying it was nearby and contained a body, which they intended to re-inter at night!

It was believed they had done this though there appeared to be no tangible evidence and the episode could have been no more than a fabrication. Furthermore, the report continued with details of a similar box, which had burst open on the northern side of Hawick, en route for Edinburgh and was found to contain the body of a man. However, relating the same story in *Round Carlisle Cross*, the local writer, James Walter Brown, tells us that the box contained the bodies of three children.

We are left with the question as to how authentic this story was? According to the *Paquet*, the broken box with its macabre contents was taken on to Edinburgh. Though the carriage had already been paid, an additional charge of twenty shillings was handed over without demur upon request, possibly by one of the medical fraternity. We are not told who examined the broken box in the first instance. Presumably someone took advantage of the embarrassing situation and profited by it.

The two men previously alluded to were then said to have been seen in different areas of Carlisle. At one inn they asked for a private room away from the main building but could not be accommodated. They had been there several times before but now appeared to have vanished upon realizing that their plans had been discovered. It was supposed that they went back to Edinburgh, since they both spoke with broad Scottish accents. A report from a Scots surgeon that he had seen someone he had known in Carlisle on a table in an Edinburgh dissecting room was the cause of additional consternation.

Over succeeding weeks, a number of more tangible incidents occurred. On the day of the first report in the *Pacquet*, the body of a Botchergate blacksmith who had been buried on 11 November 1823 turned up in St Cuthbert's churchyard. The feet were tied as though in preparation for transit. This body was carefully re-interred. It was then discovered that two other bodies had been removed from St Cuthbert's. Other graves there had been disturbed but not robbed.

A number of bodies had also been removed from their resting places in St Mary's churchyard. Public opinion became increasingly outraged and groups of volunteers were formed to watch St Cuthbert's, St Mary's and other churchyards in the city. A reward of twenty guineas was also offered by the church authorities for the apprehension and conviction of the grave robbers, a considerable amount of money in 1823. Fortunately however, no further depredations took place and gradually things settled down again in the border city.

Needless to say, with anatomists prepared to pay up to twenty guineas for a fresh corpse, it is scarcely surprising that the insidious traffic in corpses continued on elsewhere for some years, the

St Cuthbert's church and graveyard. Andrew Richardson

authorities displaying their usual lack of decision. Then finally, following the exposure of Burke and Hare in Edinburgh in 1828 with all the accompanying odium, a Select Committee of the House of Commons was at last appointed and, in 1832, necessary legislation was passed to ensure that the dead in Carlisle and elsewhere could finally rest permanently in peace.

Chapter 20

Arsenic in the Oatmeal
1847

... he made a dramatic exit, juddering and kicking wildly in the air for some time after the trap was sprung.

Following John Graham's acquittal in August 1845 on charges of poisoning his wife and father with arsenic, a write-up in one of the local papers stressed that it was too easy to obtain poison and suggested that something be done about it. This was sound thinking. If Graham wasn't guilty, then surely someone else was and had obviously procured the means without a deal of difficulty. Yet no steps appeared to have been taken to address the problem and just two years later, another man appeared in court at Carlisle charged with poisoning his wife.

On 6 August 1847, John Thompson of Union Street, Carlisle, presentable and closely shaven, appeared at Carlisle Assizes, pleading not guilty in firm tones to the charge against him. If he had any qualms at all he didn't show them, appearing as indifferent as Graham had been. Thompson's wife, Mary, had died the same agonizing death as Peggy Graham and her father-in-law. But in this instance there did at least appear a better prospect of obtaining a conviction.

Forty-two year old Thompson had only lived in Carlisle since Whitsuntide of the previous year, having moved there with his wife from Crosscanonby. The couple had originally been natives of Newcastle and Thompson still spoke with a Tyneside accent. A millwright by trade, he had obtained regular work in Carlisle but never appeared to have prospered greatly. This was evidenced by his dingy two-roomed accommodation in Union Street, one of the most socially deprived thoroughfares in the city. Not that he was there a great deal. Having been married twenty years without children, he seemingly preferred, when not at work, to frequent public houses and privately licensed drinking dens of which there were plenty in Carlisle, leaving his wife at home. It was in one of the latter, in September 1846, at the house of a weaver, Edward McBride, that he met a widow, Margaret Kane.

While there is no evidence that until then Thompson had ever been unfaithful to his wife, sufficient to say that having became involved with Kane, the plausible millwright began spinning an elaborate web of lies and make-believe to hold on to her. He posed as a widower, calling himself John Peel, and presently forged a document stating that his wife was buried at Maryport. When Kane discovered that there was a woman living with him in Union Street, he passed Mary off as nothing but a lodging house mistress while the rejected woman herself, although aware of the other woman, refused to speak ill of her husband.

To be charitable to Margaret Kane, though quickly prepared to share her bed with Thompson in the same

Union Street, Carlisle, where Mary Thompson died in agony. Carlisle Library

room where her children slept, in premises not too far from Union Street, she was probably not totally to blame. She does not appear to have been particularly bright and as well as falling prey to a number of her plausible lover's lies, clearly she had had a hard time since losing her husband seven years previously, supporting herself and three children by working in the fields and making caps. She was probably also lonely and glad to have a man back in her life and was prepared to give him the benefit of the doubt more often than she might normally have done.

Nevertheless, by May 1847, she might well have been wondering if she wasn't making a fool of herself after all? Thompson continued to spend most nights with her but unfailingly departed around 3 am to Union Street where his long-suffering wife had even begun leaving the door off the latch! Nothing had come of his fine promises to marry Kane though he still maintained that he was single. It may be that the widow now gave him an ultimatum, or that he was simply weary of leading a double life after all.

Whatever the reason, it was about now that Mary Thompson began suffering the same symptoms as Peggy Graham: sore throat, agonizing stomach pains, vomiting and thirst, which gradually intensified. Neighbours became concerned about her, while despising her husband whose adultery was known to a number of them.

A few days before her death, Mary Thompson called at the home of a neighbour, Ann Dixon, with swollen eyes and flushed cheeks, saying she had felt so sick that she had almost vomited in the street. Before leaving, she gave Mrs Dixon a piece of veal pie. The neighbour, her daughter and niece, all sampled this and were violently sick as a result. John Thompson was informed and promptly claimed that he too had felt disordered after sampling the same pie! Had he read up on the Graham case, of such comparatively recent vintage?

On the following day, Thursday, 27 May, anxious neighbours sent for Thompson at his workplace and insisted that he get a doctor as his wife was worse, with a temperature and a burning throat. The husband took his time but eventually a Dr Mortimer attended. He prescribed soda powders and Thompson returned to work. On 28 May he was urgently requested to get the doctor again which he did but to no avail. Nothing appeared to relieve the patient.

That night the sick woman's condition took a final downward turn. During the early hours of Saturday, 29 May, she died, threshing the bedclothes in agony while her husband stood by the bedside, fresh from his nightly sojourn with Margaret Kane.

He didn't appear affected by his wife's death at all. Nor did he question the doctor's decision to notify the coroner. Meanwhile, the dingy flat was in a chaotic state. As well as the disordered bed from which the corpse had recently been removed, there were pots and bowls everywhere, caked with the remains of rice, gruel and vomit, as well as a brimming chamber pot. The doctor advised that none of the vessels should be removed or their contents thrown out. John Thompson thought differently.

That same evening, the inquest took place. This was adjourned, affording the bereaved husband the opportunity to have the place cleaned up. When the cleaner refused to touch the pots, bowls and chamber pot, he emptied and scrubbed them out himself after she had gone.

Upon being informed that his wife's body was likely to be opened up, he may have consoled himself that there was now little evidence left to go on and between continuing to visit Kane, arranged to sell off his furniture. But the police were busy too. Following a referral from the coroner, they searched the flat and took samples from the occupant's waistcoats and spare trousers. They then sealed off the flat and refused to allow its tenant back in to remove a bag of oatmeal. Finally, on 8 June 1847, the affable adulterer was taken into custody.

The police action was justified. At the subsequent post mortem on Mary Thompson, no less than twenty-eight grains of arsenic had been discovered in her stomach. There was also arsenic in her intestines, though otherwise, she had been a healthy woman. Fifty grains of arsenic were detected overall. Arsenic had also been discovered in Thompson's pockets and in the oatmeal. The Tyneside expatriate was in deep trouble.

At the subsequent trial there were none of the anomalies, which had spared John Graham the noose. All told, forty witnesses were to hand, including the unhappy Margaret Kane. None of the neighbours called were inclined to speak well of Thompson. Many confirmed Mary Thompson's agonizing decline, others her husband's adultery, and his attempts to dispose of vital evidence.

The remains of the veal pie had been thrown onto the communal midden and couldn't be traced, but the clothing and the oatmeal had of themselves yielded more than sufficient to convict the man in the dock. The key witness was one William Graham, who confirmed that Thompson had purchased poison around three weeks before his wife's death, giving a false address and saying he wanted it to poison rats. But a neighbour living on the same landing as Thompson testified that there were no rats on the premises to poison. Instead, the arsenic had obviously been mixed in the oatmeal and other food with the unfortunate wife in mind.

It only took the jury fifteen minutes to reach a verdict of guilty. Even as Baron Pollock was putting on the black cap, Thompson was shouting his innocence but the following morning, possibly realizing no one believed him, he made a full confession to the gaol chaplain, choosing to blame Margaret Kane for his predicament.

His execution on market day, 21 August 1847, on the east wall of Carlisle Gaol drew one of the largest crowds ever and he made a dramatic exit, juddering and kicking wildly in the air for some time after the trap was sprung. But then death came and presently he was cut down and buried within the precincts of the gaol like others before him.

The scene of the crime itself stood for almost a century more but was finally demolished in 1930 under a slum clearance scheme. It has been known as Rydal Street ever since and it is doubtful if most locals now have any knowledge of the tragic deed which occurred thereabouts almost 160 years ago.

Chapter 21

A Rope's end for a Rogue 1803

Alas, dishonesty was too deeply ingrained in him.

Of all the smooth rogues who came to the attention of the law in nineteenth century Cumberland, the best known was probably John Hatfield. Yet it is for his shabby treatment of a local beauty, Mary Robinson of Buttermere, that he is now best remembered.

Much of the story of this plausible adventurer belongs more in the eighteenth than the nineteenth century. He only arrived in Cumberland towards the end of his days in 1802. It has also been remarked by one writer that Mary was less of a beauty at the time of her betrayal than the story suggests. Notwithstanding, the story handed down has enough about it to confirm that Hatfield was nothing if he was not given to foul deeds, even with years of his life shrouded in obscurity. Whether or not he merited being hanged is more debatable. It may be that he simply tried the patience of too many people in the end, including the Cumbrians.

We aren't even sure of his age. He was said to be forty-four years old when he was hanged at Carlisle for forgery in 1803. Yet while one source has it that he was born about 1758, which would confirm this, another tells us that he was born earlier, about the middle of the eighteenth century, which is probably nearer the mark as he married his first victim around 1771 or 1772.

John Hatfield, a plausible rogue. Carlisle Library

What we do know is that he was born at Mottram in Longdendale, Cheshire, into a humble household. In an age of those who had either too much or too little, Hatfield decided he preferred the former category. Being soon at odds with his lowly family, he left home and commenced work as a commercial traveller in linen goods. He had all the attributes for such a career being literate, endowed with good looks and physique, smooth manners and a convincing tongue. It was about now that he entered upon a career of roguery for the first time.

Having became acquainted with a young woman on his patch, supposedly a farmer's daughter, he learnt that she was in reality the illegitimate daughter of Lord Robert Manners and was to receive £1,000 upon her marriage, provided the intended husband met with the father's approval. Hatfield lost no time in ingratiating himself with all concerned. The marriage took place and he received £1,500, a huge sum in the early 1770s. Forsaking wife and work, Hatfield promptly took off for London, living like a gentleman until he had squandered every penny of the marriage portion while posing as a member of the affluent Rutland family. He then had little choice but to return north to his wife. Nothing is really known of his life for the next ten years except that three daughters were born.

He then deserted his wife and family, the wife dying shortly afterwards, possibly of want and neglect. On this second occasion, back in London, he was presently arrested for debts totalling £160 and locked up in King's Bench Prison. Here he continued to lie and boast and began cultivating an impressionable prison visitor, a clergyman, who approached the Duke of Rutland on his behalf. The duke, having some vague knowledge of Hatfield through Lord Manners, proceeded to pay the £160 and the rogue was released!

With persistent arrogance over succeeding years, Hatfield continued to pursue his career of deceit and victimization, first in Ireland, then back in England, though much of this period is obscure until 1792 when he arrived in Scarborough, posing as a prospective MP and boasting once more of his Rutland connections. However, his debts were mounting again and he was destined to languish for seven years a prisoner in Scarborough, unable to raise the money to purchase his freedom. Finally he prevailed upon another gullible young woman, a Miss Nation, who paid his creditors, had him released from prison and became his second wife.

The couple commenced married life in Devonshire and were soon blessed with two children. It might have been thought that Hatfield would have been grateful for the former Miss Nation's support and endeavoured to return to more honest pursuits from now onwards. Alas, dishonesty was too deeply ingrained in him. He continued with his career of deceit and it was only a matter of time before he abandoned his second family and took off on his travels again, which finally brought him to Cumberland and his squalid end.

His career has been dealt with at some length to apprise the reader of the kind of man Hatfield really was. There was little romantic about him. He was no more than a crooked rogue without scruples who wasn't averse to preying on anyone he felt might assist him in pursuing his grandiose lifestyle, throwing them aside when it suited him. He wasn't necessarily violent or threatening, simply a conman without conscience who had almost forgotten he was doing wrong. We can read of his likes in any newspaper today. They are foul and despicable but a not uncommon breed. It was only when Hatfield reached Cumberland and, in tandem with fraud and forgery, embarked upon the exploitation of a woman who had had something of a reputation as a local beauty in her own isolated community, touching the hearts and minds of the local population to an exaggerated degree, that he over-reached himself to his final detriment.

Typical of the man, he arrived at Keswick in July 1802 in a horse-drawn carriage, claiming to be one Alexander Augustus Hope, Colonel of the 14th Regiment of Foot, MP and brother of the Earl of Hopetoun. Affable and smooth as ever, he soon became a favourite in local society, even while there remained those who thought him a trifle coarse for a man of breeding.

It wasn't long before he had become acquainted with yet another young woman of some wealth who was holidaying in the area with her guardians. He proposed marriage, though of course he was already wed. His proposal was accepted and he continued to keep up the pretence of being Colonel Hope, franking letters by that name and receiving the same, a fraud upon the Post Office and still a capital offence though this didn't appear to worry him. Nevertheless, his latest conquest and those protecting her interests gradually became uncertain, requiring further proof of his standing. This Hatfield couldn't supply of course. It was while he dallied over this that he met Mary of Buttermere during a fishing excursion to the lake.

Mary Robinson was the daughter of a local innkeeper who also farmed his own land. The family probably weren't too well off but a cut above the average. By this time Mary was twenty-five years old. Her beauty had been extolled ten years before by the writer, Joseph Palmer. The book concerned had had a wide circulation and the image of the beautiful maid had stuck. Ten years further on, more recent mention of Mary as being gap-toothed and broad in the beam may have been true enough and for some reason she still hadn't found a husband. Hatfield soon won her over in any case, probably with an eye to her wedding portion, though the smooth scoundrel might well have been no less than fifty-two years of age, albeit still endowed with charm and good looks. On 2 October 1802 the couple were married in Lorton Church, with Hatfield the bigamist continuing to pose as Colonel Hope. But this time he had gone too far.

Such a romantic event quickly found its way into the newspapers, some of which reached relatives of the real Colonel Hope in Scotland. They knew that the colonel was, at that time, in Austria and took up the matter. Shortly afterwards, Hatfield was apprehended and committed to the care of a constable. Incredibly, when he asked if he could be allowed to continue fishing, his request was granted. Not surprisingly, he promptly absconded, but left behind a dressing

Mary Robinson, sketched from life in 1800. Carlisle Library

case in which Mary discovered papers bearing his real name and marital state as well as his Devonshire address.

This was a useful clue but it was in south Wales where he was eventually arrested, now posing as one Luder Henry. Upon failing to maintain this deception, it was only a short time before he was committed to the Cumberland Assizes, charged with falsely posing as an MP and franking and posting letters thereby, in order to avoid the cost of postage. There were other charges, of forgery and bigamy, but these were set aside, there already being sufficient evidence of wrongdoing.

Hatfield was tried in Carlisle Town Hall on 15 August 1803. It took little time for the jury to return with a verdict of guilty of forgery and sentence of death was pronounced the following day. It has been said that the jury of Cumbrians was reluctant to see him hanged for merely forging a frank on an envelope. But his treatment of Mary Robinson hardened their hearts though it was still not expected that the conman would hang. However, no reprieve came and demonstrating surprising dignity, Hatfield was hanged on 3 September 1803 on Carlisle Sands.

Mary Robinson in 1803. Carlisle Library

He left behind a wife and family as well as a degraded Mary
Robinson, with fewer prospects it seemed than when he had first met
her. But unlike his deserted wife and children, assistance was
forthcoming for Mary. A public subscription was raised from which
she benefited substantially. She became the subject of ballads and
plays, married a farmer and died in comfortable circumstances in
1834.

Chapter 22

A Girl well used to Children 1881

She was charged with the wilful murder ... by putting her in a pool of mud and water and holding her there until she was dead ...

The tragic murder of a six-month old baby at Sprunston Farm, Durdar in 1881 was one of the worst crimes committed in nineteenth century Cumberland. The death was not only horrific, but compounded by the fact that the perpetrator, Margaret Messenger, was only fourteen years old at the time and the only female in the county to be sentenced to death. Added to this there was another infant who died at the farm while in Messenger's care, for whose death she is believed to have later admitted responsibility.

At the onset, no one could have anticipated the tragedy to come. Mr and Mrs John Palliser had hired Margaret Messenger on 9 June 1881. They had been farming at Sprunston for three years and were comparatively young people with three children, Margaret and Mark aged five and two years respectively, and Elsie aged six months. With the farm taking up so much of their time, they required a domestic servant cum nanny to assist with the housework and the children. Messenger, of Howrigg, Wigton, came well recommended by her mother who had emphasized that the strong-looking, not unattractive teenager was well used to children, being the second eldest in a family of six who had virtually brought up one of her younger siblings. She appeared just the kind of person the Pallisers were looking for.

The new girl settled in well and the children appeared to like her. Though of sullen disposition on occasions, this was deemed of no great importance. She was only reprimanded once, for teasing the children. The Pallisers liked and trusted her and all appeared well but any complacency was to be short lived. On 25 June, Messenger was left in charge of Mark, but a short time later the two year old

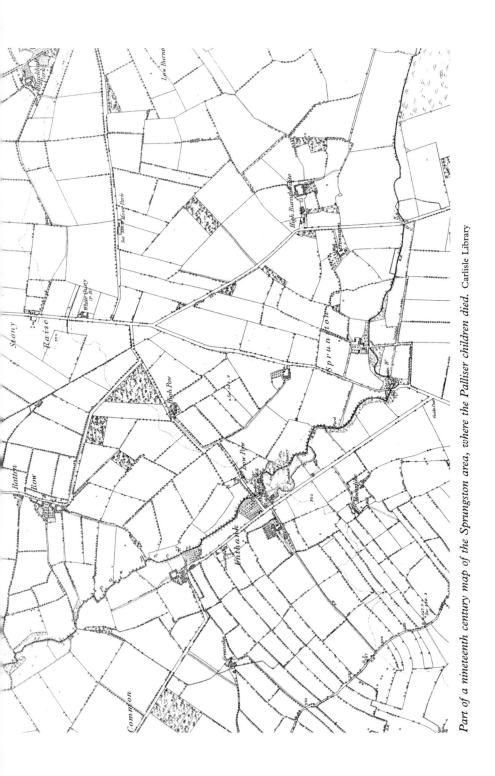

Part of a nineteenth century map of the Sprungston area, where the Palliser children died. Carlisle Library

disappeared and was discovered to have drowned in the farm well. It was the nanny who made a show of discovering the body and it is to the detriment of the authorities that she was not questioned more closely at the time. Instead, a verdict of accidental drowning was quickly returned. When Messenger blithely remarked that they wouldn't need to clean little Mark's clogs any more, no one took offence. Nor was she apparently taken to task for negligence in her supervision of the child.

Indeed, no sooner was the child buried than the nanny was left in complete charge of both remaining children. Sprunston Farm, lying no more than six miles west of Carlisle, was within easy reach of the city's market and both parents set off for there on 2 July, determined to carry on as normal. No doubt they were still grieving over the death of their only son and did caution Messenger to be additionally vigilant in the care of Margaret and Elsie, but it might still have been more appropriate if Mrs Palliser had stayed behind in this instance. However, she didn't; the result was to be another tragedy.

The couple were scarcely gone before the nanny cried out that the baby was missing. The hired lad, George Haffen, was working in an adjoining field and hurried to the scene. Margaret Palliser said that a man had taken Elsie. A seemingly troubled Margaret Messenger confirmed this. Haffen thought they were pulling his leg and returned to his work. But a short time later he glanced towards the house and saw the nanny carrying the child's inert body. Now appreciating that something could be seriously wrong after all, he raced to a nearby farm and sought the assistance of Jane Storey, the farmer's wife. She followed him back and taking the child, attempted to revive it, but Elsie was already dead, her mouth full of soil. Messenger said that a big man with a cap on had taken the child from her.

Jane Storey was a forthright woman and no doubt the death of Mark Palliser was still fresh in her mind. She challenged the girl who had stood by showing no emotion whatsoever while she had attempted vainly to bring the infant back to life. The teenager protested and said she was not telling lies; she was telling the truth.

By this time it was early afternoon. Both the police and the parents had been sent for. The latter arrived back fairly quickly but were too distraught to handle the situation. Jane Storey's husband, John, had also arrived on the scene, a man equally as forthright as his wife. Messenger had spoken of finding Elsie face down in a bog with a stone upon her head. It was John Storey who went to the bog, which was close to the well. He discovered footprints all around it and a large stone. The footprints were small and appeared to be those of a girl. There was only one such person on the property Storey was aware of. That was Margaret Messenger.

While waiting for the police he questioned the teenager. She now alleged the abductor was a tall man with a straw hat on. The farmer wasn't satisfied and went in harder. Messenger changed tack and said she had been seated on a log nursing Elsie. She had dosed off and awoken to find the infant gone. Storey retorted that the six-month old child couldn't have got from her knee and as far away as the bog. He took the girl there and showed her the footprints and accused her of telling lies. Finally Messenger began crying and said she would tell 'all the truth'. John Storey said she would tell it to those who would soon be there, namely the law.

Superintendent Douglas Sempill reached the farm some time afterwards. Storey showed him the footprints. The superintendent promptly ordered casts to be made. He then questioned Margaret Messenger closely, who responded with what were felt to be more blatant lies. No further time was wasted. She was charged with the wilful murder of Elsie Palliser by putting her in a pool of mud and water and holding her there until she was dead, at a place in the bog below the well.

Messenger protested but was instructed to dress herself appropriately prior to accompanying Superintendent Sempill to Carlisle. In her bedroom with Mrs Storey, who had been delegated to keep an eye on her, she finally made a confession of sorts: 'I did it myself and no one helped me.' Sempill was called upstairs and the teenager repeated this to him. Shortly afterwards, she was on her way to Carlisle Gaol.

It was quickly confirmed that Elsie Palliser had died as a result of being choked with mud and that as the observant John Storey had anticipated, the footprints in the bog matched Messenger's clogs. The stone alleged to have been on the little girl's head had been brought from some distance away and was of considerable size, but a fourteen year old could have carried it.

All this and the girl's admission to the Storeys and Sempill appeared to confirm her guilt. But at her trial the following November she chose to plead not guilty. This availed her nothing. The trial itself was a short one, with both the prosecution and the defence equally at a loss as to why the teenage murderess had acted as she had done. There could only be one sentence in 1881 under the circumstances, but it should be added that the fate of Mark Palliser was never mentioned at all at the trial. If it had been, the issue of unsoundness of mind might have been raised, thereby avoiding the mandatory death sentence, which Mr Justice Kay proceeded to pass with great emotion.

On the other hand, there could never really have been any question of hanging a fourteen year old girl in 1881, though many might not have grieved unduly had such a sentence been carried out in this instance. What happened instead was that a psychiatrist from Broadmoor, Dr Orange, was finally called in, who interviewed the condemned girl at some length. He found her chatty and polite to all about her, enjoying her food and sleeping well. She was keeping in touch with her family and had become an enthusiastic letter writer. She never did give the psychiatrist any specific reason for her crime but appeared to have seen most of those about her as enemies or spies. She is also said to have confessed to the murder of Mark Palliser at this time, by throwing him into the well.

Perhaps unfortunately, Dr Orange's conclusions as to her actual state of mind were not made public but she was seen as a candidate for either Parkhurst or Broadmoor. Subsequently reprieved, she received a life sentence instead. Following an extended period of detention, she was released and returned to Cumberland. There she settled in the Thursby area, a lonely eccentric figure, becoming a staunch churchgoer. She lived a long life, finally dying in the early 1950s.

Chapter 23

A Shameful Stain
1746

Some were buried on the spot; the heads of others were placed on the city gates and remained there twenty years.

Over the centuries as we have seen, Carlisle and the area surrounding it didn't have an easy time. The Scots were usually the greatest threat. Their constant incursions over the border all too often left devastation in their wake, even while the English could be equally rapacious on occasions.

Following the union of the crowns in the early seventeenth century the situation as a whole began to ease, with the two countries operating increasingly as one and with the misfits of the debatable lands on the wane. Nonetheless, things began to tilt dangerously again with the vagaries of Charles I, leading to the siege of Carlisle and the depredations of Cromwell's troops.

A number of uneasy years followed. Few appeared concerned when the last Stuart monarch, James II, was finally driven into exile in 1688 and replaced by William and Mary who ushered in greater stability.

Unfortunately however, the Stuarts still had their Jacobite adherents, primarily on the northern side of the border. These would be the ringleaders in two rebellions, ultimately leading to a shameful stain on Cumberland's character, which involved the barbaric executions or ill treatment, or both, of many who never seriously sought to rebel in the first instance.

The first rebellion in 1715 was fairly innocuous, following the advent of the first Hanoverian monarch, George I. Scottish troops advanced as far as Longtown where momentarily they halted. They decided not to assail Carlisle, badly defended though it was, but came eventually to Brampton where they proclaimed James II's son and namesake, King, under the title of James III.

By this time the invaders must have became aware that very few Cumbrians were prepared to support them. They continued on as far as Preston but the heart had already gone out of the campaign and on 14 November they surrendered to General Willis. That same month, the leaders were tried in the town hall at Carlisle. Death sentences on twenty-five of them were imposed but never implemented. Others were discharged for want of proceedings. The whole affair fizzled out.

It was a totally different state of affairs thirty years later in 1745 when Prince Charles Edward, grandson of James II, landed in Scotland from France. He rallied many of the clans to his banner though, from the onset, the clansmen themselves appear to have had little or no say in the matter. A number of the larger clans including the Sutherlands and Campbells never rose at all, their leaders probably having the sense to realize that the rebellion was a lost cause before it had begun.

At first, the dashing young prince did appear to present a formidable threat, to the extent that the reigning Hanoverian monarch, George II, had packed a bag as a precaution. He needn't have worried. By this time most of the English had accepted the man they knew as German Geordie and some had even named their sons after him. Unfortunately, being so close to the Scottish border, Carlisle was once again in a less favourable situation. The city walls were falling into decay, defended only by a few hundred untrained militia who, upon learning that no relief could be expected, promptly departed.

Meanwhile, following their creditable victory at Prestonpans, the Highlanders drove south. Coming eventually to Stanwix, they placed their cannon on the bank there but never fired a shot. The undefended city had little choice but to surrender and James III was proclaimed at Carlisle Cross. Prince Charlie himself made a majestic entry into the city on 18 November 1845 led by 100 pipers, taking up residence in a house standing on the site now occupied by Marks and Spencer.

Carlisle possibly suffered less under Scottish occupation than anticipated though the occupiers helped themselves liberally to arms and horses, both within and around the city, before leaving a small garrison in place and departing south, commandeering hay and oats in the Penrith area en route. They left behind if anything, a volatile population, some of whom made trouble for the Carlisle garrison, took a number of prisoners and ultimately joined up with the government forces of General Wade.

As the Scots proceeded southwards, they met with ever diminishing support and advanced no further than Derby before turning back, coming under increasing attack from hostile Cumbrians as they approached Carlisle again. They were back in the city by 19 December after an eventual set-to with the Duke of Cumberland at Clifton. They departed again almost immediately on 21 December leaving a garrison of a mere 400, a mixture of Scots, English and French. Shortly before this, the invaders had contemplated blowing the city to pieces to delay the Duke's advance over the border. In fact the Duke presently fired on the place himself from Stanwix and Newtown, making a complete mess but forcing the castle garrison to surrender which it did, on 30 December 1745.

For the moment, the captured men were confined in Carlisle Cathedral until 10 January 1746, when they were sent on to Lancaster and Chester. In the meantime, Charles Edward Stuart continued to retreat north with his main army, pursued by the Duke of Cumberland. The Jacobites achieved a noteworthy victory against General Hawley at Falkirk on 17 January but this would be their final triumph. At Culloden, on 16 April, outnumbered and badly organized, they were defeated and their young leader fled, eventually finding his way back to France and dying there many years later in 1788, a despised drunkard.

At least he died in his own bed. Those he had left behind were less fortunate. From the onset, cruelty and degradation were the norm in Carlisle, as elsewhere. A foretaste of things to come had been evidenced by the treatment meted out to the 400 men, taken into custody at the end of 1745. Within days they were being made ready for their journey south. George Gill Mounsey affords us a stark description of this event in his classic work *Occupation of Carlisle in 1745*:

> *The officers were placed on horseback, their legs tied under the bellies of their horses, their arms pinioned so as to afford them barely the power of holding the bridle, each horse was tied to the tail of the one before it. The privates were on foot, each man's arms tied the whole marching two abreast fastened to a rope ranging between them. The Governor, Hamilton, went first, his horse led by a Dragoon with drawn sword; then followed the officers, and Dragoons in the rear. The foot were preceded by two Dragoons, one of whom held the rope to which the prisoners were attached, the whole were followed up by a body of Dragoons. In the melancholy procession which thus filed through the ancient archway of the English gate were many who but six short weeks before that, had marched out of it flushed with victory and inspired by the highest hopes. Miserable as their present condition was, the retrospect must have aggravated their misery by awakening the most appalling anticipations of the future. They were now in the hands*

of the Government, alarmed and incensed by their former temporary success.

The man who continued to dominate the grizzly scene was the Duke of Cumberland, better remembered as Butcher Cumberland. Duke William Augustus (1721–1765) was no exceptional commander. He owed his position to the fact that he was the second son of George II and when Hawley fouled up at Falkirk, was appointed to replace him. He had had an inconspicuous role in the War of the Austrian Succession. But then came Culloden where his army numbered about 9,000 as opposed to under 5,000 on the Jacobite side, many of the latter troops having gone off to seek food, most of them famished following failure on the part of the leadership to organize transport for rations and other supplies.

William Augustus, Duke of Cumberland. Carlisle Library

Others were exhausted after a futile manoeuvre the evening before. The prince's stubborn decision to fight on open ground unsuited to the Highlanders was the final straw. This and the untried twenty-three year old's dithering contributed to the defeat of his army at the hands of a man who would never win another battle, and whose career would end in ignominy after capitulating to the French in the Seven Years War. For the moment however, William Augustus was supreme and his appalling reprisals earned him his nickname.

This is not the place to detail all the foregoing. Sufficient to say that the majority of those of the Jacobite troops not slain in battle or later savagely bayoneted as they lay wounded in the field, were sent for trial in England. Three hundred and eighty-two arrived in Carlisle alone. In the old city, no one was discouraged from reviling and ill-using the prisoners by those in control. The Duke of Cumberland himself remained elsewhere for the moment, but his influence continued to be felt in and around Carlisle as everywhere else.

Given all the occupying troops, court officials, witnesses and others, the city itself became hopelessly overcrowded, with a shortage of accommodation and food at inflationary prices. The prisoners

Entrance to Carlisle Castle dungeons. Andrew Richardson

themselves were crowded into the primitive dungeons in Carlisle Castle with inadequate lighting, food or water. There were so many of them that the task of trying them all was considered too great for judges and juries. Eventually they were allowed to draw lots with the intention that one in twenty would be tried, whilst the remainder would be transported. Following this, the 127 indicted prisoners were set apart and allowed some time to prepare their defence. But conditions of confinement remained so cramped and primitive that this proved all but impossible.

The trials at Carlisle finally commenced in September 1846. They were a tragic farce. It was considered enough for someone merely to swear that they had seen a defendant, English or Scottish, wearing a white Jacobean rosette. This was surely calculated to bring out the worst in certain unsavoury individuals, desirous of getting back at someone they felt had previously wronged them, though a number of the prisoners pleaded guilty in any case.

Yet if some had hoped that by doing this, death on the scaffold would put a speedy end to their misery, they were wrong. Their worst ordeal was yet to come. Four hundred and twenty-three years previously, Andrew de Harcla had undergone the barbaric punishment of hanging, drawing and quartering on Harraby Hill. In eighteenth century Britain such a form of execution ought to have been a thing of the past. Sadly, nothing had changed.

Hearing this dread sentence pronounced upon him by the reactionary, Baron Parker, one of the prisoners began to weep. But another of his comrades hushed him. 'What the devil are you ashamed of?' he exclaimed. 'We shan't be tried by a Cumberland jury in the next world!' In all, ninety-six received the death sentence at Carlisle of whom thirty-one were executed. The first nine were dispatched on Harraby Hill on Saturday, 18 October 1846 at the hands of a brutish character from Hexham, William Stout, who had arranged to perform his act of butchery for twenty guineas, plus his right to the prisoners' clothing and any other articles they possessed.

Not a voice was heard in protest. Other prisoners were dispatched at Penrith and Brampton that same October. Eleven more died horrific deaths on Harraby Hill on 16 November. All are reported to have displayed the greatest fortitude. Some were buried on the spot; the heads of others were placed on the city gates and remained there twenty years. Prisoners not executed remained in abysmal confinement in the city until the late spring of 1847, ever anticipating death on the scaffold. But finally, those who had not died in prison were all transported.

The whole murky episode is now a distant part of the region's history, though thinking people locally are still prepared to admit that it reflected shamefully on Cumbria's stature at the time. England and Scotland had constantly been at war with one another in the past, and Carlisle and district had usually been in the firing line, be it as a springboard for the incursions of Edward I into Scotland, or those of

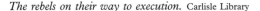

The rebels on their way to execution. Carlisle Library

Bruce and his ilk in the reverse direction, and more besides. So paranoid did the city itself become that no Scot was allowed to remain there overnight for many years. For several centuries there had also been the border reivers to contend with, although in this respect, one side of the fragile border was as infamous as the other.

Nevertheless, the scene had been changing ever since the union of the crowns. By 1745 there was much more trust between English and Scots. Unfortunately however, a residue of resentment and mistrust remained in and about the old city. This emerged more fully following Charles Edward's abortive rebellion, which a majority in the region had never expected or wanted. This brought out the worst in a number of people locally, though indeed, England's leaders as a whole were much more to blame.

On the other hand, inhuman prison conditions in Carlisle Castle, adverse decisions by Cumbrian Grand Juries and barbaric executions on Harraby Hill were not easy to expunge from the Scottish psyche and never have been, even while such excesses were also being propagated elsewhere in England at the time.

Yet on a brighter note, there were benefits from the whole depressing business too, in that with the great improvements brought about afterwards in communications as a result of General Wade's efforts, Carlisle and other places were more ready and able to benefit from the industrial revolution when it began to take hold. The city itself would never be under siege again and in less than 100 years most of the walls would be demolished, with Scots and others free to go as they pleased.

Chapter 24

In the Call of Duty
1885

... he was laid across the railway line and would probably have been decapitated ...

The Netherby three have probably merited a mention in more books on Cumbrian crime than any other local offenders. They have also been the subjects of innumerable regional newspaper articles over the years. Only recently, their crime has featured in a documentary on Border Television. More than a century after a foray into Cumberland which ended in a brutal murder, while many locals now have little if any knowledge of Lightfoot, Cass, Margaret Messenger and other home-grown killers, a majority are still acquainted with Rudge, Martin and Baker.

It isn't easy to pinpoint the reason for this. It possibly lies in the fact that Cumberland as a whole was never endowed with the same persistent villainy as many other regions of Britain following the demise of the reivers and other alien outsiders. In the opinion of one writer on crime, the region was now more likely to be associated primarily with Scottish raids and Jacobites. This was far from true as will already have been evident here. Crime remained and could be serious enough. But Carlisle and the area about it had undoubtedly become less violent with the passing of the years, even allowing for the earlier travails of the industrial revolution.

Anthony Benjamin Rudge, forty-five years old, John Martin, thirty-six, and James Baker, twenty-nine, would briefly change all that. All were professional criminals from southern England and had served various prison terms. All detested the police. Rudge and Martin were already wanted for questioning concerning the murder of two police officers prior to their arrival in Cumberland. Baker was a more thinking individual with some modicum of decency. But he was still an unrepentant crook. He carried a gun and was not to be underestimated when cornered.

The sheer ruthlessness of the trio, their determination to sweep all before them and kill as necessary to escape, during the hunt for them which ensued following a blatant jewel robbery, cannot fail to have touched the minds of many locals now generally accustomed to a more law-abiding way of life. There was also the presence of a fourth man who disappeared and was never identified. All this made for a story, which has tended, by and large, never to have grown entirely dim with time.

Yet dig beneath the veneer of sensationalism and drama, the jewel robbery, the police presence, the ensuing murder, the capture of the three villains, their trial and execution, and the true facts are a trifle more ignominious.

It all began when the London area became a trifle too hot for the threesome. Taking advantage of the rail network, they packed housebreaking equipment and revolvers and moved north to Scotland for a few months. Rudge and Martin weren't leaving much behind them. Neither had a fixed address nor regular employment, giving their occupations as dog trainer and cigar maker respectively, though Martin did also work on occasions as a bookie's runner. Baker was different in that he had a wife, Nellie, and the twosome ran a green-grocery shop in Bethnal Green. But criminality remained something they all had in common and they appear to have had a good run in Scotland burgling country houses, before moving south again and stopping off at Carlisle on 27 October 1885. Leaving their house-breaking tools at the railway station, they moved on quickly to a

Netherby Hall in 1993. Cumbrian Newspapers Ltd.

coursing event at Longtown the following day, close to the scene of their next intended robbery: Netherby Hall.

At this time it may be safe to assume that the fourth man, some local reprobate, had entered the frame and filled their minds with tales of the loot available for the taking at Netherby, so that he might later accompany them there. Netherby Hall had existed for several centuries, the family seat of a more illustrious branch of the Graham clan. Over the years the family had had their ups and downs, entering a better phase again during the mid nineteenth century with the coming into the title of Sir James Graham, both a competent administrator and politician, a contemporary of Palmerston and Russell.

Sir James died in 1861 and was succeeded by his son Frederick. The latter and his wife Hermione were well thought of locally. Yet they were still not as affluent as some might have supposed. Their home was comparatively small compared with many in the area. The prospective burglars might have done better focusing upon such grander local residences as Naworth Castle, or the Lowther residence, south of Penrith.

Nevertheless, they obviously had sufficient knowledge of Netherby to utilize a ladder and go straight to the main wing which contained Lady Graham's bedroom. Unfortunately for the gang, they were disturbed by a maid but were still able to make off with jewellery valued at around £250, a sufficient haul to spark off a police hunt for the culprits who, it was calculated, would make for Carlisle, some twelve miles to the south, via the main road from Longtown.

Information having quickly reached the local force at Carlisle by telegraph, Sergeant John Roche was sent with PC Handley to go to the suburb of Kingstown on the Longtown road. After deciding to send Handley back to watch the city railway station, Roche joined up with the local constable, Jacob Johnstone, and awaited developments. They were quickly rewarded by the sight of four figures coming towards them in the moonlight from the direction of Longtown. All were formally dressed and resembled city men as opposed to locals. Roche challenged them, only to be covered by revolvers held by the two older men who were later identified as Rudge and Martin. The twosome promptly opened fire without troubling to speak, shooting Roche in the arm then beating him brutally about the head before making off with their two companions. Johnstone chased them and was shot in the chest. The two policemen, bleeding badly, retreated to the police house.

Down the road at Morville, Handley heard the shots and had the acumen to realize what had probably occurred. He quickly recruited two local men, Armstrong and Hetherington. The foursome reached Morville shortly afterwards and though armed only with a stick, Handley challenged them. He was advised by the fourth member of the group, dressed in lighter clothing than the others, that they were sporting men and that he had been assaulted at Kingstown and wasn't prepared to cooperate further. Handley said he must detain him, whereupon both he and Baker pulled out revolvers and pointed them at the policeman and the civilian, Armstrong, while Rudge and Martin stood ominously by. The result was that Handley and his volunteers stood aside and the four criminals proceeded on their way. It had been a wise decision on the part of Handley. Now at least the police knew the kind of men they were hunting. But they didn't appear to have learnt a great deal from the experience either as time would tell.

The four miscreants had the sense to avoid the main bridge over the Eden, which they anticipated would be watched. Instead, they crossed the river by the Etterby railway bridge. Three of them were next seen by Strong, the keeper at Dalston Road Crossing, at around 2.30 am, heading towards the goods yard where presumably they intended to stow aboard a train. Strong reported the matter to PC Christopher Fortune the local beat bobby. Fortune guessed who the trespassers might be. Yet he appeared to have learnt nothing from what he must have heard to date, nor to have been instructed to go carefully. Instead, he emulated Roche and Handley, directly challenging the trio.

Suddenly a fourth man appeared and that was the last Fortune knew. Beaten unconscious, he was laid across the railway line and would probably have been decapitated had Baker not had a change of heart, returning and pushing him down the embankment. Three of the men were next seen briefly in the goods yard around 3.30 pm. By this time it was assumed the fourth man had left them. Certainly he was nowhere to be seen when they were next sighted at Calthwaite Railway Station, halfway to Penrith, at 7 pm that same day.

They must have been remarkably resilient, having committed the jewel robbery two miles north-east of Longtown, then walked all the way to Carlisle, a distance of some twelve miles in under three hours. They had then shot and assaulted the two police officers before taking a divergent route in order to safely cross the river. Having next dealt with PC Fortune, they had then apparently scouted around the goods yard for an hour before heading off towards Penrith. Their local guide and accomplice having presumably departed, they may have now taken time off for a sleep in some isolated barn or wood. But they had

From left to right: Anthony Benjamin Rudge; John Martin; James Baker; and PC Joseph Byrnes. Cumbrian Newspapers Ltd.

still walked a further nine miles before being sighted at Calthwaite Station, probably having had little or nothing to eat on the way.

It goes without saying that they must, nonetheless, have been tired by this time and less vigilant, emerging from cover to enquire about a train south. They were told there was nothing until 7.32 the following morning. No sooner were the disappointed trio out of sight than the stationmaster telegraphed the station at Plumpton, bringing the local policeman, Joseph Byrnes, into the picture.

What happened next was to result in one of Cumberland's most callous murders. The police officer discovered that the fugitives were in the local *Pack Horse Inn*, partaking of bread, cheese and beer. He knew of the manhunt and presumably what had already happened to his colleagues. So, too, did his superiors though there is no evidence that they advised any of their officers to exercise caution. Instead, PC Byrnes made the same mistake as Roche and Fortune. He challenged the trio outside the *Pack Horse* carrying only his truncheon and refused to desist. As was later revealed, he was grabbed by Rudge and Baker, shot through the head by Martin, then dragged a few yards and thrown over a wall into a field. Discovered, one and a half hours later, he died soon afterwards.

Following this atrocity, the wanted men were seen hurrying along the railway line towards Penrith around 10 pm. They then vanished again until observed scrambling into a goods wagon by a railway guard, Christopher Geddess, some time afterwards. From then on it was civilians who took the lead. A telegraph message was flashed along the line to Tebay and a crowd of railwaymen gathered there. The threesome made a dash for it when the train halted but a chase ensued. Rudge and Martin were both knocked down unceremoniously by railway employees; their weapons were taken, the Netherby jewels recovered, and they were firmly secured. Baker, the more cunning and agile of the three, got as far as Lancaster on another train where he alighted and hid near the station. But he then made the mistake of emerging and asking a railway guard about a train to Crewe. He was recognized and secured by railway staff and joined his two accomplices in Carlisle Gaol that same day.

It was doubtful if the three would have been taken so easily had they not been so tired. Should the railwaymen have even been allowed to risk their lives? There is no evidence that they were discouraged from doing so. But without them, would the villains have been caught at all? Probably they would in the end, given the magnitude of their crime.

The fact remained, however, that the police force was still badly manned and poorly paid. Communication between the regional forces was abysmal and expectations of individual officers far too high. One wonders how many more courageous men like PC Byrnes might have died before justice was done in this case, had the railwaymen not risked their lives. Nor was the fourth man ever identified or caught and no one seemed to really care. To this day, no one knows who he was.

Memorial stone to PC Byrnes at Plumpton, Cumbria. Andrew Richardson

Cumberland was, in fact, euphoric. The villains were in custody, everyone could sleep safely in their beds again and, of equal importance, Lady Graham had her jewellery back!

Unfortunately the price paid had been heavy, as was evident when the trial of the three prisoners finally commenced on 18 January 1886. Sergeant Roche had been rendered virtually immobile. PC Johnstone, fortunate to be alive, had to give his evidence seated in a chair. PC Fortune had no less than nineteen wounds and would never work again. PC Byrnes was dead and the best the authorities could offer his widow was a place for her children in an orphanage, following the execution of the three perpetrators on 8 February 1886.

It was a sad ending for many but hopefully some lessons were learnt along the way too. Indeed, the situation would be handled totally differently in these times. Meanwhile, the case continued to grip the imagination of the public. It was a popular local play as late as October 1938 and the three criminals even made it into Madame Tussaud's Waxworks for a time.

Paradoxically, the memorial stone in Plumpton commemorating the bravery of PC Byrnes is now neglected. But who knows when there may be yet another book or documentary, even though the case has long since slipped from the attention of those elsewhere.

Chapter 25

Death of a Gamekeeper 1849

His neckerchief was drawn so tight that it was buried in his neck.

Thomas Davidson had been a gamekeeper for Sir James Graham of Netherby for twenty years in the remote and wild district of Bewcastle, some twenty-three miles northeast of Carlisle. A man advanced in years but still alert and robust, he was no friend of the poaching fraternity though their threats did not appear to trouble him. On Thursday, 8 November 1849, he left home to make his usual rounds but by nightfall had not returned.

Concerned workmates and local farmers formed a party to search for him. Finally, at about 10 am on the following Saturday morning, they found his body about two miles from his home. He was dead, lying face down, arms folded under his body. His stick lay beside him. His neckerchief was drawn so tight that it was buried in his neck. Blood had flowed from his mouth and nose. He appeared to have died from violent strangulation.

Superintendent Sabbage of the Cumbrian Police had been tardy in collecting John Graham's clothing for forensic examination four years earlier. Upon now being alerted, he moved faster in this instance, going straight to the scene of the gamekeeper's death. He noted a mark on Davidson's abdomen, suggesting that this could be the foot or knee of an assailant. The dead man's throat bore a number of marks made by fingernails, while the footprints of several different people were discovered nearby. Unfortunately, the rain had obliterated these to an extent, but there was still sufficient evidence to suggest foul play.

A post mortem having confirmed cause of death, it was but a short step to drawing up a list of possible culprits. A key suspect became twenty-four year old Joseph Hogg, a local poacher. Three weeks previously he had been fined at Carlisle upon the evidence of Davidson for shooting without a game certificate. Later he had been heard to make a threat against the gamekeeper. His boon companion was his cousin, a shady individual, thirty-five year old Nichol Hogg. Another Bewcastle man who kept company with them was twenty-four year old Andrew Turnbull. But whereas Joseph Hogg was single, Nichol parted from his wife and neither man was in regular employment. Turnbull had a young wife and appeared happily married. He was also gainfully employed as a husbandman.

It took only a short time to locate two of the suspects, Joseph Hogg and Andrew Turnbull, and summon them to the inquest, which commenced the following Monday morning at Carlisle. Nichol Hogg at that time was missing from his usual haunts. The younger Hogg was duly cautioned that he was under suspicion and not required to answer any questions which might incriminate him. This didn't appear to concern the suspect. He took the oath and blandly stated that on the day prior to Davidson's disappearance he had been out shooting alone, that he had seen Andrew Turnbull briefly that day but not since then, that he had slept at his father's house on Wednesday night, sharing a bed with his cousin, Nichol, and that they remained in the house throughout the following day with his mother and sister dressing fish hooks. He denied having seen Thomas Davidson since their day in court and accounted for a recent scratch on his face by saying that he had got it while shooting in a wood. A bloodstain had already been discovered on his trouser knee, which he had also explained away. He gave his evidence clearly and confidently.

However, Andrew Turnbull had a rather different tale to tell. His home was only half a mile away from that of the first witness, and he stated that he had been with him for several hours on Wednesday in search of game to shoot, each having a gun. Presently Nichol Hogg had joined them. He also had a firearm. The trio finally parted company around 3 pm and he, Turnbull, did not see them again. He claimed he had not been out of his house on Wednesday evening or on Thursday, but that Joseph Hogg had visited his house on Sunday afternoon and sat with him for an hour after the police called.

Joseph Hogg's sister, Ann, then gave evidence. Though Joseph normally lived alone in a one-roomed shack, he did spend time at his parent's house. His sister swore that he had only been absent from there about a quarter of an hour on the Thursday. She finally admitted too that Nichol Hogg had slept there on the Wednesday night, that Turnbull had called upon him and that Nichol Hogg had left the house about 9 am on Thursday but came back between 12 and 1 pm.

Ellen Hogg, the mother of Joseph, at first denied that Nichol Hogg had been in the house at all the previous week except once, but finally admitted that he had slept there several nights including Wednesday and Thursday.

The dead man's son, Joseph Davidson, confirmed that on the Thursday evening he was at Joseph Hogg's home. The latter was not there but his fourteen year old sister was, with his own six year old daughter. This concluded the Monday proceedings which were adjourned until the following day.

That night, Nichol Hogg was discovered in Rickergate, one of Carlisle's seamier areas, where it appeared he had been since the preceding Friday. At the resumed inquest on Tuesday morning he gave evidence. He stated that after sleeping with cousin Joseph on Wednesday night, he and Joseph went out on Thursday morning and called upon Andrew Turnbull. They all went out shooting down the area of Lineside and into Cumcrook Wood, returning between 6 and 7 pm, not meeting any other person. They shot two woodcocks and two snipes and took them to Carlisle the following Saturday.

He was followed by another local witness, who said he had taken two brace of grouse and other game to sell at Carlisle for Joseph Hogg that same Saturday.

All in all, there had been a lot of contradictory evidence from members of a close-knit family and their acquaintances, endowed with their own brand of low cunning, who came from a remote community where everyone knew everybody else.

The jury may well have been pondering all this and more, until their task was put on hold before the Tuesday proceedings were well under way. Word came that Andrew Turnbull had made a full confession to Superintendent Sabbage which had been taken down in writing. The content of this was not immediately made public. But it was obviously serious enough to warrant the two Hoggs and Turnbull being taken into custody, following adjournment of the inquest until Monday, 26 November.

By this time the Bewcastle murder, as it was already being described, had became headline news and everyone awaited further developments with great interest. Upon the resumption of the inquest, Turnbull was a much greater object of attention than before, a young man, slightly above ordinary height and powerfully made, with bushy hair and whiskers meeting around the chin. But his face was pale and haggard and he looked totally dejected, as though deeply regretting the events, which had brought him to his present pass. He was examined first. His second testimony was a sorry catalogue of deviance, hatred and brutality.

He claimed that on 8 November at about 7.30 am, the two Hoggs came to his house and invited him to go poaching. Finally he agreed to go. They went to Christenbury Crag and had a few shots but brought nothing down. On the way there, Joseph Hogg had spoken

The lonely region of Bewcastle. Andrew Richardson

of putting an end to old Tom if they came upon him and of he, Turnbull, assisting. He had declined but said that if anything did happen and didn't endanger his own life, he would say nothing. Eventually their luck turned and they shot two brace of grouse, a black cock and a woodcock. He took four shillings for his share of the birds. They wended their way homewards and about 3.30 pm, encountered Tom Davidson.

The three of them all began running but then Joseph Hogg shouted for Turnbull to stop which he did. Thereupon Hogg went for Davidson and a fight ensued. The younger man threw the gamekeeper down. Nichol Hogg assisted and soon it was over. The younger Hogg cursed Turnbull for his faint-hearted attitude for he had begun trembling, then rifled the gamekeeper's pockets and took out his purse. It contained three sovereigns and fifteen half crowns. He put the purse back, leaving in it a £1 note and some silver. Turnbull accepted a sovereign and five half crowns as his share. Then they went home, after making up a tale to cover themselves. However, he had been so upset that he had told his wife of the murder.

Questioned as to what he had done with his share of Davidson's money, he said he had paid a tailor and drank away four shillings of it. He had also bought currants, flour and a cheese and was left with four shillings.

Jemima Turnbull, his wife, confirmed her husband's confession and that Joseph Hogg had said it would be a happy death if he should be hanged for the gamekeeper's murder. She admitted to hiding her husband's boots afterwards.

Recalled again, Joseph's mother confirmed that he had been away from home on the Thursday and that she had given her son's clothing and guns to Sabbage, but was more evasive as to where the grouse had gone. His sister, Ann, was not inclined to render full assistance either, stating that she couldn't confirm her brother's departure on the Thursday, saying sullenly that they didn't have a clock, but finally said it was after her mother got up.

What did emerge in particular was how badly liked Davidson had been, in a community which saw poaching as a way of life. The dead man's son said Turnbull had also threatened him.

Finally the jury had heard everything and the coroner summed up, carefully reiterating the circumstances under which the deceased had met his death, but at the hands of whom precisely?

If the jury remained uncertain themselves, they gave no indication of this, returning a verdict of wilful murder against Joseph Hogg, Nichol Hogg and Andrew Turnbull by strangulation with the deceased's neckerchief. The trio were returned to Carlisle Gaol to await their trial.

The final outcome was not yet a foregone conclusion of course, even with Turnbull's statement to assist the prosecution. The jury's verdict indicated this, more so given that the impressions of all three men's footprints had been confirmed as being those close to the scene of the crime, and hadn't Turnbull already lied once?

The forthcoming trial appeared likely to be very well attended indeed, but then came a dramatic event, changing everything. Andrew Turnbull would not be appearing again. On the night of 28 November 1849 he hanged himself in his cell, leaving three messages scrawled on the walls.

The first was below the window. It read:

The two Hoggs are guilty. I am innocent. I will not come in the hands of man.

The second was above the fireplace:

I commit my soul to God that gave it. Take my body to my father's burying place.

The third was above his bed and addressed to his wife:

My dear, you and I was lovely but I am torn from thy breast. Do not weep for me. Jemma, my dearest, my heart's delight and treasure, I am innocent. I die with pleasure. We meet again with pleasure. Beware of bad company. My parents are not to blame. They did their duty. Adieu, my dear friends.

The result of this event was the subsequent acquittal of Joseph and Nichol Hogg. As the judge put it most succinctly:

An ordinary accomplice is a very bad man to rely upon at any time but what is the state of the case when he is called? He is put into the witness box; you see him, you hear what he says and again observe his manner; he is subject to cross-examination and the effect of the questions may tell materially upon him. This accomplice you have never seen but you know he has sworn falsely how then can you put faith in his statements without having the opportunity to examine him? I say, is it reasonable to act upon his testimony?

The public at large may have found the final verdict a trifle difficult to take. But no doubt the two remaining defendants were ecstatic that their fellow poacher's departure had spared them what could otherwise have ended in another triple hanging.

Chapter 26

Death under Mysterious Circumstances 1896

... a number of letters from the dead girl were found in his pockets.

On Carlisle Cemetery there is a tombstone erected to the memory of a local girl, Eleanor Coulthard who, it is claimed, met her death under mysterious circumstances in April 1896. She died near Brungerley, Clitheroe, but the case is included here as both the girl, and the man originally suspected of causing her death, were Cumbrians. Indeed, at the time she died, the sixteen year old was said to be homesick for Carlisle and district, which was eventually seen as a salient point in the possible cause of her death.

Carlisle cemetary, where Eleanor Coulthard lies buried. Andrew Richardson

Eleanor Coulthard was a sturdy, full-faced girl, not exceptionally beautiful, but with all the hopes and feelings of one her age. She was the daughter of Mr and Mrs Robert Coulthard of Orchard Street, Carlisle and grew up in the border city. Like many another in those times, domestic service was seen as the best occupation she could aspire to and in February 1896, the teenager travelled to Lancashire to take up employment with Mr and Mrs John Chorlton of Chatburn, near Clitheroe.

Given that there must have been similar employment closer to home, it seems surprising that a teenage girl should have been required to travel so far away from her family. On the other hand, insofar as her new mistress was concerned, she appeared to settle in very well, proving to be conscientious, civil and honest. One Monday, the following April, she came to Mrs Chorlton around 3.30 pm and asked permission to go out and meet a friend from Carlisle. Her employer agreed without demur.

That was to be the last time she saw Eleanor Coulthard alive. The next day the girl's body was found in the River Ribble a short distance away. It was virtually unmarked and there was nothing to suggest that she might not have met her end through suicide or an accident. Nevertheless, the police immediately instigated enquiries and were not slow in unearthing a number of suspicious facts.

Early on the preceding Monday morning around 4.45, Sergeant Holmes of the local force had encountered a twenty-four year old slightly built man named Henry Bertram Starr. He recalled that the same man had had a lodging house voucher issued to him at the nearby police station the previous evening. When he now asked Starr why he was about so early, he said he didn't want to be seen in the lodging house, explaining that he was more concerned to pawn his overcoat because he needed money, having a young lady to meet at Chatburn that night. He had seemingly met her the previous evening but she had had no money then though had promised to have some tonight. Upon being plied further by the sergeant, he revealed that she was a young lady from Carlisle and had come to be a servant at Chatburn. He explained that he himself was theatrical, a conjurer, singer and musician, but had left his company at Carlisle.

Feeling sympathetically disposed towards Starr, who appears to have had the ability to engender goodwill on occasions, the sergeant gave him a shilling and advised that he go to Blackburn, which wasn't far away. There he said were a number of theatres, any one of which might require an entertainer. Starr appeared more concerned about finding a public house open, claiming to be dying for a drink, but the two men parted on amicable enough terms.

That night, at 12.15, Holmes met Starr again. The latter had come from the direction of the river. He was intoxicated and wet from the waist down, claiming to have been drinking all day and then having fallen over the bridge into the river. He spoke of having pawned his jacket for five shillings and of spending the lot, in addition to the sergeant's shilling, with the exception of three pence. He claimed not to have met the young woman from Carlisle after all due to his drinking. He then staggered off towards a nearby lodging house.

Holmes was again on duty when Eleanor Coulthard's body was recovered the following day, and was present when Starr was interviewed afterwards on a routine basis at his lodgings. Following close questioning, he now admitted to having met the girl around 7 pm the previous evening, and indeed, had been seeking her at her place of work just prior to that, as was to be confirmed by Mrs Chorlton. He said that they had gone for a walk and quarrelled, because she wouldn't go away with him, and that he had left her standing on the footbridge over the river.

He went on to give a clear description of Eleanor and also furnished her Carlisle address. Upon being confronted by news of the girl's death he turned away and stared out of the window, registering no emotion. Asked if he could give any explanation as to how she got into the river he responded negatively, but then said: 'When I come to remember, she did say something in that letter about committing suicide.' Shortly afterwards he was taken to the police station and charged on suspicion with having caused the death by drowning of Eleanor Coulthard.

Having been searched, a number of letters from the dead girl were found in his pockets. They were love letters and she had obviously been deeply enamoured of him. They appeared to have first met in Carlisle when Starr, a native of Maryport, had been acting as a book canvasser for a local firm of publishers. Starr, eight years older, had obviously captivated the impressionable youngster and when she had gone to Chatburn had followed her and had recently wanted her to run away with him. However, this she had refused to do, probably remaining under the sway of her family and employer to some extent.

Starr appeared to have persisted. This was made clear at the inquest when a witness, a Major Smith, testified that he had seen the couple twice on the fatal evening near the river, the first time about 8.40 and then later, around 10.25. He heard the girl say 'no' several times and more than once she asked her companion to go, though the twosome appeared to remain friendly before disappearing from his sight.

Evidence of the couple's seemingly cordial relationship was presently confirmed by another witness, Margaret Smith, a Chatburn girl who, with her sister, had been with Eleanor on the Sunday evening prior to her death. The trio had come upon Starr unexpectedly but the teenager had introduced him and the couple had gone off, chatting pleasantly, with Starr at that time talking of making for Belfast.

The girl's employer for her part had spoken of Eleanor Coulthard as being bright and cheerful, even while Starr did imply during the inquest that she had hated Chatburn and wanted to get away from the place. There was, of course, only his word for that though the girl did clearly miss not being with him as many a lovesick young girl might. Of greater relevance, Mrs Chorlton was sure Eleanor Coulthard was neither the excitable nor suicidal type.

This was not quite as others saw it. Both at the inquest and the subsequent magistrates hearing, the police surgeon persisted in his view that there being no water in the girl's stomach, he felt that she had either had no inclination to respite, or had been prevented from doing so. Bearing in mind that there had been no external marks of violence, he tended to be of the opinion that the first likelihood applied; in fact, that she had committed suicide. In one of her letters to Starr, she had certainly said that if he went away without saying goodbye she would do something desperate to herself. But again of course, this could have been no more than the cry of an immature girl.

In his summing up, the coroner didn't spare Starr. He felt the latter had done the girl wrong, keeping her out late and sullying her reputation. But he emphasized too that it was insufficiently clear as to whether or not he had pushed her into the river, or how he had got wet, and that the matter was best left to the police to take any further steps they might consider necessary. The jury chose to go against this advice and return a verdict of wilful murder. This inevitably brought Starr before the magistrates' bench. They committed him for trial but in the light of all that had gone before, it came as no great surprise that when he eventually appeared at Liverpool Assizes, he was acquitted for want of sufficient evidence.

Eleanor Coulthard had already been laid to rest in Carlisle Cemetery and there the matter might have ended, despite lingering doubts on the part of some, particularly the girl's immediate family. Then seven years later there occurred an event blowing everything wide open again.

Following his acquittal at Liverpool, Starr had disappeared from the scene for a time. Little is really known of his ongoing way of life until November 1902 when he was introduced to one Mary Hannah Blagg, whom he married in March 1903. The couple went to live with

Eleanor Coulthard's gravestone.
Steve White

relatives of the wife in Blackpool. All went well for a few months until Starr began to drink, bringing out a violent streak in him, which his wife and her extended family found intolerable.

The result was that Starr went to live with an aunt but continued to visit his wife on occasions and an uneasy relationship prevailed, until the volatile husband informed Mary Hannah that he had been unfaithful to her. She then showed him the door but, upon giving birth to his child on 21 August, a reconciliation of sorts took place. This was only of short duration. Starr's conduct continued to be irresponsible and his wife took the child and returned to live with her mother.

A pattern not unfamiliar to most social agencies now rapidly took shape, with the frustrated husband threatening that if his wife would not live with him, he would have custody of their child. Mrs Starr countered by taking him to court and he was ordered to pay six shillings maintenance per week. This was unacceptable to a man who never appears to have been very stable. Following the court hearing on 23 November he was seen loitering outside his wife's home and heard repeating again and again: 'I'll do it, I'll do it.'

Early on the morning of 24 November, the young wife was in the kitchen preparing breakfast when her mother suddenly heard the girl screaming. She raced downstairs and saw Starr hacking wildly at his wife with a bread knife. She went to her daughter's aid and Starr attacked her, slashing her face and hand before racing out through the door. A doctor was called but the younger woman had sustained so many wounds that she was already dead.

Starr was meanwhile behaving in a manner ominously reminiscent of that which he had displayed around the time of Eleanor Coulthard's death, going from bar to bar and drinking uncontrollably. Finally having decided to wash his bloodstained hands in a public toilet, he was arrested there and charged with wilful murder.

He was put on trial the following month making no attempt to deny the crime. His defence was that heavy drinking had brought on delirium tremens and that he had murdered his wife in a drunken frenzy. If he had hoped this might move the court at all he was to be disappointed. There could be no question of sparing him, the judge describing the crime as a frightful murder, both premeditated and brutal. There was no recommendation for mercy from the jury and the perpetrator was executed in Walton Gaol before the year was out, going to his death, it was said, with profound resignation.

Even with death staring him in the face, however, he never did confess to the murder of the unfortunate girl lying in Carlisle Cemetery. Was he innocent of the crime? He had been acquitted, of course, but in the light of his wife's recent fate, many could surely be forgiven for wondering if the circumstances surrounding Eleanor Coulthard's death had been so mysterious after all?

Chapter 27

The Madness of Michael Carr
1898

He ... began beating the helpless old man with one of his sticks ...

Longtown's Hallburn Workhouse was a sad establishment like others of its kind, no more than a receptacle for the old and needy. In the summer of 1898 it was business as usual with eighteen men and nine women in residence, the establishment short on staff as was normally the case. On 1 June a seventy-nine year old inmate was brutally murdered. If nothing else, the case does serve to illustrate just how hazardous such places could be for residents and staff alike.

On the night of the crime, the workhouse manager was doing his final round of the ward for the infirm, which held seven patients ranging downwards from 106 years old. All were asleep except sixty-one year old Michael Carr, an odd character at best, who was talking loudly, saying he only wanted to get to sleep. There appeared nothing to stop him but such was the nature of the man. He was given to mindless complaining but eventually did fall silent.

Carr's history was a trifle contrary. Though listed as a labourer who read and wrote imperfectly, he was said to have been a schoolteacher in his younger days. Probably he had been no more than a classroom volunteer or a monitor for when new schools and new teaching methods began to proliferate, he became unemployed. The only work he could find afterwards was stone breaking and he continued at this for some years, a bad-tempered morose individual. This was scarcely the best temperament for someone who had aspired to teach children, though there may once have been a better side to him.

Much of this became of little consequence in any case, when he was admitted on 23 May 1898 to the workhouse under a relieving officer's order. Since he had become a prey to bronchitis and was now a cripple, dependent on two heavy sticks, he was admitted to the hospital ward. He had been no problem at the onset but gradually became more vocal and restless. What no one appeared very concerned

Longtown as it is today. Andrew Richardson

about at the time was that Michael Carr also had a history of psychiatric illness and had had a number of admissions to Garlands Asylum in the past. But since he had harmed no one and it was obvious how infirm he had become, it was perhaps felt that he was no risk to anyone any more.

In a bed close to that of Carr lay seventy-nine year old James Nichol, another local individual who had known better days. He was a former draper who had eventually settled in London but finally returned to Longtown, where he had been admitted to the work-house as a pauper. Things had improved for him when his son died and left him a legacy. He had promptly taken his discharge from the workhouse to live back in Longtown. Sadly, the money was all too quickly spent and he was forced to return to the workhouse in 1897. He was now crippled and blind but normally docile and manageable.

Manager Dawes satisfied himself that everything was in order and left the ward around 11 pm, returning to his quarters. His peace was to be short-lived. Within an hour, he heard loud shouting. He emerged to find the seventy-five year old ward monitor, Alexander Bell, standing outside. Bell advised him of an awful mess involving Carr and Nichol.

The two men went to the ward. Carr was seated on a commode clutching his sticks. When challenged by the manager he struck out but the latter closed with him, and another elderly patient, George Graham, noting that Carr appeared to be getting the better of the scuffle, struck the man over the head with his own stick, partly stunning him. Other infirm patients looked on helplessly but it was now possible to get Carr into a straitjacket and send for the doctor.

The ward itself resembled a slaughterhouse. As Bell told it, he had seen Carr leave the ward then return shortly afterwards but he hadn't gone back to his own bed. He went to Nichol's instead and ordered the sleeping occupant to get out of it, saying it was his. He ignored Bell's protestations and began beating the helpless old man with one of his sticks, by the light of the solitary oil lamp. Soon there was blood everywhere, on the bedclothes, the stick, the walls, the floor and the ceiling. Nichol being infirm to begin with, died quickly, his face battered in and his right arm broken. Carr, though only about five feet seven inches tall, was very powerfully built from the waist up and the older man never stood a chance.

When Dr McKirdy arrived, all he could do was certify the victim dead. It was left to the police to take Carr into custody and he was remanded to Carlisle Gaol. The inevitable inquest quickly followed at the workhouse. The patient, Graham, said that for two days past he had noted something strange in Carr's manner. Unfortunately, he had not reported this. It was a pity those with more responsibility hadn't been as observant but with the establishment being so short staffed, this was probably scarcely surprising.

It appeared from Dr McKirdy's evidence that since the event, Carr had quietened down, though he had flown into a rage when his scalp was being dressed following the blow from Graham's stick. When being charged, he had merely said: 'All right.'

The coroner spoke of a shocking and painful case and praised Bell and Graham for their prompt action. He didn't feel either could have done more to try and save the victim's life. His main concern now was to determine whether it was murder or manslaughter because Carr had not been attempting to defend himself and neither had Nichol done anything to agitate him.

The jury had no such concerns. A verdict of wilful murder against Carr was pronounced and George Graham was rightly commended for his action in stunning the prisoner. Ironically enough, today Graham might have been in trouble himself for taking such an action, but things were more clear-cut in 1898!

The next step involved the magistrate's bench at Longtown. A remand was requested and Carr, his head still bandaged, listening afresh to the verdict of wilful murder queried vaguely: 'Is that your verdict? Did you give a verdict of that sort against me?' He continued to ramble, despite attempts to quieten him, but was soon on his way back to Carlisle Gaol.

Carr's trial commenced early the following month before Lord Justice Bruce. Little is clear-cut in law but in this instance, the outcome appeared almost a foregone conclusion. When asked to plead the prisoner said: 'I know nothing about the man. I never saw him in my life that I'm aware of. I know nothing about it, nothing about it whatever.'

The sole witness was Dr Archibald Campbell of Garlands Asylum. The psychiatrist said he had known Carr for twenty-eight years. He had had him in Garlands five times between 1870 and 1888. There had been no re-admissions since then and he had not interviewed him again until the previous month but while in Garlands, Carr had suffered from mania and was extremely violent. During the onset of these attacks he was dangerous to others. The prisoner's father had died in the asylum and an uncle had committed suicide. Having seen Carr again in June, he did not consider him sane and hardly thought he even understood why he was on trial. He didn't think Carr's state of mind was such as to allow him to defend himself properly. Thereupon Lord Justice Bruce asked the prisoner if he wished to say anything to the jury. Carr's response left no doubt in anyone's mind as to his mental state. 'No, Sir,' he said. 'I've no question to put to anyone. They all know about their own business. I know about mine and the Almighty knows the remainder.'

The judge addressed the jury, saying that they had heard the evidence of Dr Campbell who had had the opportunity of assessing Carr's mental state. If they thought that Carr was not fit to plead it would be their duty to say so. Such being the case, he would have to order the prisoner to be detained in a lunatic asylum during Her Majesty's Pleasure.

The jury lost no time in finding Carr unfit to plead and the judge passed sentence accordingly. Afterwards he asked Dawes to stay behind and praised his bravery and decision, but felt it was desirable that the manager should have adequate assistance in the event of a repeat of this nature. There is nothing on record to tell us that His Lordship's thinking on the matter received the attention it clearly deserved.

Chapter 28

A Clergyman in Court
1851

He became so deranged that it was impossible for the local magistrates to consider bail ...

The Reverend Joseph Smith scarcely gave the impression of being a pillar of spiritual support to anyone when he appeared at the Cumberland Assizes, Carlisle, on 6 August 1851 charged with manslaughter. Smith cut a pathetic figure, appearing close to collapse. He was still probably wondering how he had got into his present predicament.

Following some time as a curate with the Reverend John Fawcett, Vicar of St Cuthbert's, Carlisle, where he was said to have been devoted to his duties, Joseph Smith had been posted to the parish of Walton, near Brampton. There was a stark contrast between the bustling downtown environment from which he had came and his new parish, with its acres of lonely countryside. Nor did the large rambling vicarage enchant him, even though standing as it did in Walton Village, it was rather less isolated than some writers made it out to be. The living itself was yet another Perpetual Curacy with a stipend of only £120. The nervous little man had scarcely bettered himself but simply had to go where his bishop sent him. In the event, he had been there a full fifteen years when the offence occurred.

From the onset he endeavoured to make the best of things and contrived to become reasonably popular with his new parishioners who did not ask a great deal of him. But the mid-nineteenth century also saw an ever increasing rise in rural crime and Joseph Smith noted this. He felt especially vulnerable because the vicarage stood in its own grounds and was exposed on all sides. Moreover, he was the only man in it, being responsible for his wife, two female servants and five children. Not only did he suffer from nervous debility, he was also frail and short sighted. He determined to covertly purchase some means of defence.

Walton church. Andrew Richardson

This wasn't too difficult to do. He went to a gunsmith in Carlisle in November 1850 and purchased a brace of pistols but these weren't to his liking. He therefore returned and bought a six-barrelled revolving pistol, a huge clumsy weapon but one which pleased him better and he placed it in a drawer, not anticipating that he would have to use it, but feeling better for having it to hand.

Such was the state of play on Wednesday, 16 April 1851 when a new player appeared on the stage. William Armstrong was a thirty-eight year old farmer and landowner of some means with a wife and young family, who lived at Sorbie Trees Farm, some seventeen miles north-west of Brampton. He was a totally different type to the frail, nervous curate in Walton vicarage, being a man of impressive stature, with looks and personality to match. Passing years may have served to elevate his persona to exaggerated heights but there is no reason to believe that he was not a man's man. He was honest, cheerful and obliging to all those about him, although at times, like many another in those days, he drank more than was good for him.

On 16 April he rode to Brampton as he occasionally did and attended to some business with a solicitor. It being market day, he afterwards joined with friends and acquaintances and a considerable amount of alcohol was consumed in the town's hostelries. Some attempted to persuade him to spend the night at Brampton, it being now fairly late. But he had other business the following morning at

Canonbie and eventually left the town the worse for drink at around 9 pm with a friend and neighbour, William Elliot, the two men striking off along the Longtown road.

Armstrong's horse was a fast animal; he soon left Elliot behind but only rode a couple of miles before halting at an inn by the crossroads leading to Walton. Here Elliot caught up with him. They went into the inn and drank there with another neighbour until around 11 pm. This left Armstrong more intoxicated than ever, though he was said to be capable of riding and walking. Their onward route lying through Walton, the trio set off in that direction but the Sorbie Trees man again forged ahead and was soon lost along the road.

Passing through Walton around 11.30, his two companions saw no sign of him. He hadn't spoken of breaking his journey so they assumed he had simply got well ahead of them and carried on homewards alone. In fact, William Armstrong had undergone a change of mind and they would never see him alive again.

Why Armstrong decided to break his journey and call at Walton vicarage remains uncertain. What was known was that Ann Glendinning, a former servant of his father and then of him, had recently taken up employment at the vicarage. Armstrong had been heard to say that he would like Ann Glendinning back working for him. Recently he was known to have spoken with her in Walton and to have stood her a drink. Now in his fuddled state, it was assumed he had decided to call on her.

If such was the case he had misjudged the time for such a visit. Nor could he have known the state of mind of the man in the vicarage. But he carried on, dismounting and tethering his horse at the vicarage gates before walking up the drive to the north side of the house where the front door was situated. It was a bright moonlit night though that side of the house was deep in shadow.

In the meantime, the Reverend Smith was preparing to check the building over, ensuring everything was secure before retiring to bed. Already his nerves were thoroughly on edge. The children had been put to bed early but the youngest child had experienced some kind of nightmare, screaming incessantly. Peace was eventually restored but not before everything had became disorganized. The evening prayer ritual had been upset and the adults later than usual getting to bed.

Finally however, the clergyman was left alone downstairs. In a subsequent statement he related how he began his security check, examining windows, shutters and doors. His nerves remained frayed but everything appeared in order. Then suddenly there arose a violent repetitive knocking which appeared to come from the study. Fearfully he entered the room and slammed down the iron bar normally securing the shuttered window. The noise ceased but he wasn't satisfied.

Taking out the huge revolving pistol from its place in the drawer and grasping a small lantern, he crept to the front door, then throwing it open fired wildly into the gloom. He was to claim to have seen nobody and given that his sight was defective, this could well have been true. Nevertheless, he didn't loiter, rushing inside again and slamming the door shut. But then upon reflecting that he may have hurt someone, he apparently plucked up the courage to open the door again and by the light of his lantern, looked about but saw nothing and retired to bed, relieved he said, that he appeared to have frightened the intruder or intruders away.

Ann Glendinning, the apparent cause of the impromptu visit, went to bed around 11 pm in a room above the study. She spoke of falling asleep and of waking again about 11.30 pm, roused by what she thought was something heavy falling. She then heard the front door being closed before falling asleep once more. She knew nothing of Armstrong's presence at the time. The other servant, Sarah Blackwell, also heard a similar sound. No one else in the house appeared to hear anything, all continuing to sleep soundly.

It was a different state of affairs the following morning. A milkmaid came upon the body of William Armstrong lying dead behind the front gate. His steed had also been discovered grazing out on the road, its saddle and bridle still in place.

The body was removed to the local inn. Here the inquest took place, often the standard venue for such proceedings in those days. A post mortem had already revealed that Armstrong had been shot three times, twice in the back and once in the abdomen. The latter shot had proved fatal. It appeared he had retreated to his horse then collapsed and died.

After hearing what evidence was available from the distraught clergyman and others, the coroner addressed the jury. In essence, he opined: 'If Mr Armstrong's conduct, however innocent, was such as to cause the householder to misconstrue his intention, it would be stretching the law to make that man criminally responsible. Some allowance ought to be made for a man whose fears are suddenly aroused at a late hour in the circumstances described. In your decision, consider that Mr Smith was not in a position to weigh the circumstances, but was called upon without warning at the dead hour of the night, whilst under an impression that an enemy was at the door.'

The result was that the jury found the Reverend Smith guilty of manslaughter and the Cumbrian public at large appeared to go along with this at the time. The wretched clergyman did not. He became so deranged that it was impossible for the local magistrates to consider bail and he was taken into custody. Eventually, application was made to a judge in London who granted Smith bail in his own recognisance of £400 and two sureties, each of £200, from a local JP and a vicar from Brampton.

Some months elapsed. Finally, on 6 August, the matter came to court before Mr Baron Platt, where the prisoner was indicted for the manslaughter of William Armstrong of Sorbie Trees at the village of Walton, on 16 April 1851, by shooting him with a pistol loaded with powder and bullet.

The evidence was much as it had been at the inquest but it was the final part of the judge's summing up which probably determined the outcome when he stated, in sum, that in the first place, one of the first principles of British Law was that every man had a right to defend his possessions, more especially when attacked by a midnight aggressor. Though it was said that it was requisite some caution should be used, there were some places in which one couldn't apply very strictly, the rule of caution. It was undeniable that the deceased had no business at the vicarage at that unreasonable hour of the night, and that his death was brought about by his own imprudent act. It was for the jury to say whether at the time, Mr Smith had genuine belief that robbers

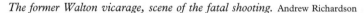

The former Walton vicarage, scene of the fatal shooting. Andrew Richardson

were breaking in. It would make no difference that no robbers were actually breaking into the house for if a man conducted himself in a manner as to lead to that belief, it was precisely the same in effect, as if this had actually been the case.

The jury obviously accepted all this for they returned with a verdict of not guilty. Whereupon there arose loud hissing from the public gallery and the judge had to call for silence, reminding the offenders that the court was not a theatre! The clergyman had meanwhile sunk to his knees in prayer upon hearing the verdict. He was then assisted from the dock and, accompanied by his loyal wife, returned to Walton.

In the normal order of things, the public as a whole may well have gone along with such a verdict. This has been evidenced in much more recent times of course, when there has been hostile response in respect of those pilloried after defending their property. But in Smith's case it was felt there were still too many unanswered questions. The clergyman's nervous debility tended to be dismissed as of no great consequence in an age when many still had to struggle simply to survive. As many saw it, why hadn't Smith first sought to attempt to discover the reason for the sudden knocking if only from within the safety of his house? Instead, he had opened the front door and blazed away indiscriminately. Afterwards he claimed to have searched the grounds but he couldn't have made a very thorough search! It had been a moonlit night and Armstrong had been lying only a few yards away. How could he have missed him? In the opinion of most locals, the injured man might still have been alive at the time and could have been saved.

The Reverend Smith may still have hoped that his troubles would end now, that he could put the past behind him and continue in his living, ministering to the people of Walton parish and gradually recover his equilibrium. Such was not to be. Apart from anything else, William Armstrong had been a much more popular man than him and though the coroner's summing up had been accepted more or less without criticism, the judge's was not, denoting as it did, the final word. Life was made unbearable for Smith at Walton. Soon he moved elsewhere and no more was heard of him.

This case also reflects perhaps, the grass roots attitude to religion by many in Cumberland and elsewhere in those times. Victorian Britain was noted worldwide for its strictness of Sunday observance. Rich and poor alike were prevailed upon to follow a godly way of life. Some of the greatest men and women of the period were deeply religious: Charles Kingsley, David Livingstone, Florence Nightingale, Josephine Butler. Victorian novels continued to contain more reference to clergymen than doctors or scientists. In the established schools, each day began with a prayer.

Many did fervently believe and drew strength from their faith. But they were quick to detect class distinction too and weren't clergymen establishment figures? All in all, the verdict probably was the right one but insofar as many in and around Carlisle, Brampton and Walton were concerned, Joseph Smith got off because he was a clergyman and not a very commendable one at that and ought to have been dealt with much more severely.

Chapter 29

After the Races
1826

She ... called him a robber and a murderer and asked if he intended to kill her.

On a Saturday early in October 1826, Sarah Draper took the road home from Penrith. The races had earlier concluded there. She had been employed on the course in some menial capacity and was tired out but still reluctant to return to her lodgings in Carlisle. Since the previous year she had been living with sixty year old Jane Myers in Ritson's Lane. This was situated in the Irishgate Brow area, similar to nearby Rickergate with the same cramped sub-standard properties.

She didn't dislike Jane Myers. Unfortunately however, the woman was a chronic drunkard. Obviously she had seen better days and had once had a hard working husband who was a chimney sweep. After he had died a few years previously, she had inherited the house owned by him in Ritson's Lane. It was not palatial but did have four rooms. The widow had promptly let three of these and lived in the fourth, a not uncommon practice in the old border city where accommodation remained at a premium. In order to get additional money to feed her drink habit, she put lodgers up in her own room as well. This was where Sarah Draper slept, on a shake-down, while her landlady slept with her lodger, forty-two year old John Ray, in a double bed in the same room.

It was John Ray who was the problem insofar as Sarah was concerned. He drank as hard as Jane Myers and when drunk, had a tendency to take offence at any personal comment, often becoming physically violent in the process. But Jane didn't help things either for she would goad him and bring trouble upon herself.

When Sarah Draper reached her lodgings in Ritson's Lane shortly before 10 pm, she found Myers and Ray there drinking with two local men. When one of the visitors asked for more whisky, Jane Myers poured out half a pint, all she had left. This was quickly gone and the visitor asked for a refill. Myers refused, saying she wanted to go to bed. Ray butted in and said he would go out and get whatever was required. The older woman said he shouldn't go out as it was too late in the evening but Ray would have none of it. Money was finally produced by Myers but then withdrawn, whereupon the two visitors departed.

Shortly afterwards, Draper, Myers and Ray all retired for the night. Sarah Draper lay on her shake-down but was kept awake by the bickering of her drunken companions. Ray was accusing Myers of not trusting him with her money to buy whisky and making him appear untrustworthy before others. Jane Myers retaliated verbally and Ray struck her. She fell out of the bed and he kicked her repeatedly. Afterwards she lay on the bed and called him a robber and a murderer and asked if he intended to kill her.

It was a familiar pattern. The couple had been quarrelling, parting and coming together again since the beginning of their relationship but this time things appeared more serious. Ray shouted that she would make him neither a robber nor a thief. He grabbed her feet, pulled her off the bed and dragged her across the stone floor, her head beating upon it, then hit her again. When Sarah Draper attempted to interfere, Ray pushed her away and threatened her too. He carried on beating the older woman while Draper retreated beneath her blankets. He threatened Myers repeatedly and was almost choking her in her chair. She was only saved from further punishment by a visit from a couple with whom the bully departed to seek more drink.

He was back at eight o'clock the following morning, confronting Jane Myers and asking her how she felt after the licking he had given her, adding that what he had given her last night would be nothing to what he would give her if he had not already done it effectively. He then departed with the pick of his miserable possessions. Such was the level that people like Myers and Ray lived at on Irishgate Brow. Most would have considered she was well rid of such a creature. Unfortunately, though he did not come back on this occasion, he appeared to have left a residue of suffering.

On the day following the beating, the abused woman got up for half an hour in the afternoon but then stayed in her bed for three days. She complained of a pain in her side and of headaches and ate little. She then appeared to improve and was seen drunk again on two occasions, her need for alcohol remaining unabated. She attended at the local dispensary but continued to spit blood from the time of her final run-in with Ray. This loss of blood only ceased a day or two before she died, some three weeks following the beating.

The Irishgate Brow area of Carlisle in former times, once one of the more socially deprived areas of the city. Carlisle Library

The death led to an inquest. An exceedingly apprehensive Ray attended, having been brought from Brampton, protesting his innocence as might have been expected. He was even more shaken when a verdict of murder was returned against him, it being decided that death had been occasioned by a fever, produced from the wounds inflicted on the dead woman's person.

Eventually, the charge was reduced to one of manslaughter. But Ray knew he could still face a heavy sentence if found guilty when his trial commenced before Baron Hullock in early March 1827. One of the most damning witnesses was Sarah Draper who held nothing back and, of course, had witnessed the entire affray. On the other hand, when cross-examined by the defence, she did admit that Jane Myers was in the habit of getting drunk whenever she could and had been drunk on the night in question, cursing Ray before he hit her, while he several times bade her to be silent beforehand. Further prompted, she admitted that Jane was so drunk she could scarcely stand and may have fallen from the effects of liquor as much as from the blows, her nose and mouth having been bleeding when she lay on the floor. She was it seemed, also apt to cry out aloud when drunk, whether hurt or not, and had became gradually worse after getting drunk the week following the beating.

Dorothy Sewell, a neighbour of the dead woman, also recalled events surrounding the beating. She had heard Jane Myers cry out. She then saw Ray lean out of the window and heard him say: 'I've been serving the old bitch out. I'm the man that can do my work effectively!' Next day she had noted that the victim's face and left shoulder were both black. But she believed these bruises could have been caused by a fall as both face and shoulder were grazed and her neighbour had been tipsy at the time. She had seen Myers regularly afterwards. She had appeared to be in good health until she took to her bed and died.

Robert Graham, Apothecary to the Carlisle Dispensary, felt the bruises were the cause of Jane Myers' death. Her right eye had been black and she had pain in her side. She had laboured under a severe pleurisy. While he felt that pleurisy proceeded from many causes, blows frequently occasioned it. If there had been any previous inflammation, drinking would increase it. But in his judgement, bruises without drinking or bad treatment would not have occasioned death.

The very worst of people can occasionally get someone to speak well of them. Ray had, in fact, been able to call upon several witnesses favourably disposed towards him although whether this was as a result of self-preservation on their part, in the kind of brutish environment in which they all lived, was difficult to say.

Be this as it may, John Cowen, a neighbour of the prisoner, spoke of him as a civil man, even while it emerged that the twosome had exchanged the minimum of words in their day-to-day lives. Cowen had probably known the deceased woman better, mentioning that she had spoken to him of selling Ray's remaining kit for three shillings and getting a good fuddle out of it. Another neighbour, John Armstrong, said Ray had saved his son's life, going down into a well to get the boy out when no one else would. Two women spoke up for him, though the second added that she had heard different stories about him.

In the light of at least some of this, it seemed there might be a better side to the drunken misfit after all, as there is to most people. Jane Myers couldn't have been the easiest person to deal with either, scolding and belittling a man who wasn't the brightest.

On the other hand, the woman was dead, following upon the actions of the accused and had surely deserved better, whether or not the blows had been the prime cause of her death? This was also the concern of Baron Hullock and he made it clear in his summing up.

He felt that the real question was whether or not Jane Myers would have died if she hadn't continued drinking after the injury. If she would not have died from the result of her bad usage, Ray could not be found guilty. That he had beaten her brutally, however, was not in doubt and there was no excuse for this. He himself could see no reason for her death but the blows, except getting drunk. From Ray's remarks it was clear he intended to injure her and confirmed this the following morning. If the blows had promoted her death, Ray was guilty of manslaughter.

The jury retired and deliberated for an hour, before returning with a verdict of guilty. Passing sentence of two years with hard labour in the new Carlisle Gaol, the judge was obviously in full accord with the verdict, remarking that Ray's crime approached as close to murder as could be conceived and that he had even questioned whether or not he should have transported him.

Chapter 30

Drunken or Deranged?
1898

... he had no recollection of what he had done on 11 August. His defence was now one of insanity.

he record of Dr John Archibald Campbell was impressive. After receiving his education at Edinburgh Academy, he proceeded to Glasgow University to study psychiatric medicine under Professors Thompson and Lister. He passed out in 1865 and his rise proceeded unabated. He was employed first at the Argyll Asylum but was there only a short time before leaving Scotland to take up an appointment at Durham County Asylum as an Assistant Medical Officer. Not unlike some modern whiz kid, he was only there a few months before moving yet again, to become Medical Superintendent at Garlands Asylum early in 1867. There he remained for the next thirty-one years.

At the time of his appointment, Garlands had been open less than a decade, a huge institutional establishment situated to the south of Carlisle. It had accommodation for up to 1,000 patients, its catchments area taking in most of Cumberland and Westmorland. The origins of the asylum had been in keeping with nineteenth century thinking in that the majority of the mentally afflicted were seen as being better off in institutional care, allowing families to function more competently in the new industrial climate. The result was that such places had become a growth industry, continuing to proliferate over the decades.

On the other hand, they were also designed to be self-sufficient and did generally pay their way, while also offering refuge to many who might otherwise have become vagrants or drifted into the underworld. Whether or not they necessarily possessed the medical expertise to cure many of their residents at the onset was more debatable.

In this latter respect, Campbell's success rate proved better than many. It was said that out of a regular population of 600 patients,

A wing of the former Garlands asylum. Andrew Richardson

recoveries averaged fifty per cent annually, while more than seventy per cent of men and sixty per cent of women were gainfully employed on the hospital farm, in its gardens, workshops, the laundry, kitchens, and even on the wards. Of course it could be argued that many of the inmates would have got well anyhow and those working were toiling for little more than their keep, but no one was complaining.

In addition to this, Dr Campbell, while demanding strict adherence to the rules and regulations of the establishment, was prepared to allow some additional licence to those patients who had proved themselves. He was a keen advocate of weekly dances, concerts, variety shows and lectures for the patients. He encouraged others on the outside to take an interest in Garlands and served as President of the Border Branch of the British Medical Association. He was interested in psychiatric developments overseas and contributed regularly to the literature of the profession. When it was finally announced in July 1898 that he had decided to retire, many were genuinely sorry.

But no one is perfect and in Dr Campbell's case, this would soon become apparent. No sooner was his retirement announced than within weeks, rumours began circulating, alleging his misconduct with one of the female patients. It was said that the Lunacy Committee had had the matter brought before them at a private meeting and this proved to be the case. On 18 August, the Medical Superintendent was arrested at Garlands and brought before one of the County Magistrates, charged with a serious misdemeanour. Bail was set in total at £1,000, a considerable sum in 1898, but then Dr Campbell was a not inconsiderable personality.

Ironically enough, only a fortnight previously, the Lunacy Committee had voted him a pension of £700 a year and expressed their appreciation of all his good work. He was due to retire at his own request within a week and had already booked a passage to Russia to explore the mental health scene there. Now he would be bound for the Carlisle Winter Assizes instead. What had gone wrong?

That would soon become clear. On 23 August the doctor appeared at a committal hearing. Full details were revealed. It was alleged that on 11 August he had taken a thirty-six year old female patient from the hospital laundry and into a store cupboard. The cupboard door had been left open and he had been observed in a compromising situation with the woman. The witnesses were three female members of staff. The defendant blamed drink and had spoken of suicide. Perhaps surprisingly, in the light of this, he was again allowed bail. Possibly some clandestine agreement had been reached for it then emerged that he would be watched day and night at his home.

His trial at the Assizes got under way three months later in November 1898 before Mr Justice Phillmore. The former Medical Superintendent looked pale, saying lamely that he had no recollection of what he had done on 11 August. His defence was now one of insanity.

The prosecution was immediately on the rebound, outlining the facts in detail. Incisively, it was described how the defendant had taken the retarded woman into the cupboard, which faced a window. The cupboard door wasn't closed and three laundry maids would say they had seen the accused commit the offence with which he was charged.

It was felt that at the time, he undoubtedly was intoxicated, probably the reason why he couldn't remember. But it was emphasized that intoxication was not a defence given the nature of the offence. It was further described how, after the incident, the patient had been escorted to her ward by the doctor, who made his own way out. Only later was he removed to his house from another female ward by one of his assistants, Dr Bell. Later, the Matron had made a statement to Campbell's Senior Assistant, Dr Farquherson, and the matter had been taken from there.

Examination of the witnesses commenced. The responses were exceedingly revealing. Was the accused really insane?

Jane Ritchie described how about 5 pm she had seen Dr Campbell take the patient from the laundry, down a passage and into a large empty cupboard with its open door facing a window. Through the open door she saw the prisoner begin to commit the offence with which he was charged. Her two colleagues Jessie Little and Margaret

Henderson confirmed this. They all appeared to think that he had been intoxicated at the time.

Dr Bell, questioned as to the mental condition of Dr Campbell, felt that the latter's memory was first class and that he could always do his work. On the other hand, he considered the doctor repeated himself senselessly and extravagantly and had rather too great an opinion of himself, magnifying his position and importance. He spoke of his former superior liking to speak of all the money he had made through consultations. He felt Campbell had probably exaggerated, that he was untruthfully boastful, speaking of a patient who was one of the Royal Family though there was no reason to believe this. He said Campbell was often drunk; the latter statement had been made when he was drunk, though at the Visiting Committee meetings he was sober.

On 12 August he had spoken with Campbell about the previous day's happening. The accused had remarked that if the worst came to the worst, laudanum would settle all matters, adding that he had not been in his right mind since he had had *that blow on the head*. On 19 August Campbell had told him he had given up the idea of suicide because he found that if he did it, some of his insurance policies might not be paid! Dr Bell did not feel that Campbell was insane.

Dr Farquherson, now Medical Superintendent in Campbell's place, had similar evidence to give. He spoke of how his former superior had admitted to him that no doubt he had acted foolishly but he had done nothing else and a charge of this kind was enough to make a man commit suicide. Afterwards he had accepted an attendant in his house to keep an eye on him.

Of equal significance, Farquherson spoke of a change in Campbell's behaviour during recent times. He had been more often drunk. He could do a morning's work without difficulty but in the afternoon would go into Carlisle and was then often the worse for drink. At other times he was rational and responsible. When sober he was inclined to be boastful about his capabilities. Drink accentuated these. He took more drink after the charge. He appeared to appreciate his situation and said he had the means to do away with himself but gave up on the idea. But was he mentally disturbed? Farquherson felt that a blow on the head could have a bearing and he understood that Dr Campbell had been hit on the head with a patient's clog at one time. He had also heard him say he had been called upon to consult about members of the Royal Family but he was drunk then. Possibly he was given to lies rather than being insane!

Thomas Grainger, the asylum's head attendant was called. He confirmed that he had taken charge of Dr Campbell for a week in

August. He had no reason to believe that the man's mind might be affected. He saw no delusions.

The Chairman of the Visiting Committee said that Campbell's business capacities had been remarkable. He had never seen anything to lead him to believe that the man's mind was unhinged; before this event he knew nothing of his drinking habits. Other members of the committee agreed.

This concluded the case for the prosecution. Though the defence was one of insanity, obviously no one from Garlands felt the prisoner was of unsound mind at all.

Now it was the turn of the defence. Their witnesses could well have been speaking of a different individual altogether and there were many more of them.

The first to be called was a local solicitor, G A Lightfoot. He stated that on 29 July last, at about 3.30 pm, he met Dr Campbell who showed no sign of drunkenness but drew him aside saying that they didn't know who they had living amongst them; that he had received a message from the Queen to go by special train to Windsor to examine a member of the Royal Family. He had then gone on to rationally discuss a prosecution in which he had been concerned.

Dr Hair of Carlisle deposed that he had known the prisoner many years. Over the last two years he had noticed mental deterioration in him, believing his mind to have became gradually diseased. On the day of the offence, Dr Campbell had visited him, wishing to say goodbye, saying he was going to Russia and was to be consulted by a member of the Royal Family there. He also claimed to have taken consulting rooms in London, that he had been guaranteed a fee of 300 guineas a year by the University Clubs of Glasgow and Edinburgh; more recently he had been seeing a patient in Sheffield and had received a fee of 150 guineas! The witness felt that Campbell was under delusions and that he showed no signs of drunkenness.

David Brown, a banker, stated that on 30 July, he had travelled from Lockerbie in a train with Dr Campbell who was excited and boasting about the large fees he was receiving. He had also spoken about a huge bill he had paid for a dinner. The banker concluded the man was upset in his mind. He hadn't appeared drunk.

On its own, Brown's deposition was scarcely very conclusive, but the next witness was much more convincing. Dr Norman, Medical Superintendent of Richmond Asylum, Dublin, stated that he had known Dr Campbell about fifteen years. In July 1898 he had noticed a great change in the man. At a recent meeting of the British Psychological Association in Edinburgh, the doctor had told him he had been sent for from Windsor to see a Royal personage, that the

Queen had sent a special train to Carlisle for him and that it was a grand thing to travel in a special train and have all the traffic stopped for you. Here the witness was interrupted by laughter as the banker had been. The proceedings were not without their humorous side.

But Dr Norman wasn't laughing as he went on to describe how Campbell proceeded to tell him of the offer of a knighthood, a Commissionership of Lunacy, and membership of the College of Physicians in Edinburgh, free of charge. At no time did he appear drunk but did seem out of his mind. Afterwards he had attended a dinner with Campbell at Edinburgh Conservative Club, the man lighting a cigar in the middle of the meal! Norman had later talked about all this to colleagues but no one appeared to have any tangible answer at the time.

Dr Ogilvy Ramsay of Carlisle, another colleague, said that within the last year, he noticed that Dr Campbell had become more egotistical and obstinate in his opinions. He had mentioned to Dr Farquherson that Campbell was beginning to suffer from incipient general paralysis but Farquherson would have none of this. On 11 August Dr Campbell assured him over and over again that he had been appointed Alienist Physician to the Conservative Club of Edinburgh, that he had received the honour because he was the only distinguished Scottish Alienist this side of the border and was to get a retaining fee of £300 per year. There was no evidence of drinking.

There were a number of other statements by the medical fraternity, most of them relating to Campbell's grandiose delusions. Mention was also made of his conviction that friends were plotting against him to deprive him of the titles to which he considered himself entitled. But the most penetrating deposition of all came from Dr Clouston, Superintendent of the Royal Edinburgh Asylum, who was related to the prisoner through marriage. Clouston was one of those who brought alcohol into the equation. He stated that he had no doubt Campbell had taken to drink and that this had been on the increase. On 20 July he had seen him in Edinburgh at the BPA conference and was appalled by his appearance. At the end of the conference, he and three colleagues had held a meeting to try and determine what the problem was? It ended in a draw. Two were in favour of general paralysis and two in favour of alcohol deterioration, though any plan of action appeared to have been put on hold.

Clouston also knew from Campbell's wife that he had taken to going to bed the day before the monthly committee meeting and would put his head under a tap. It seemed that his affection for his wife and only daughter had completely diminished over the previous two years. His wife had finally left him in 1897 but he was never heard to express regret or grief over that. Coulson was of the opinion that Campbell's offence was, in itself, evidence of his insanity.

Finally it was time for the counsel to address the jury again. By this time the trial had gone on for most of the day. Shee, for the defence, had little more to say. He asked the jury to come to the conclusion that the accused had delusions, given the evidence of both laymen and doctors, and that at the time the offence took place he was not responsible for his actions. Could they have any clearer evidence of the accused man's insanity than the alleged offence itself? If they acquitted him, he would probably find his way into some lunatic asylum where he would have to consort with lunatics for the rest of his life, and could they imagine a more lamentable termination than that to Dr Campbell's career?

Page, for the Crown, made play of the fact that, on one hand, witnesses saw Dr Campbell when he was at Garlands while the others saw him socially, but were not all his delusions part of the grand image he had of himself? Dr Farquherson and Dr Bell had no illusions about this but still felt that the more grandiose delusions were linked primarily to his drunkenness. The only other delusion was that he had been defrauded out of a title, but were any of these delusions evidence of a deranged personality?

Mr Justice Phillmore in his summing up stressed that the jury must first consider the act committed by the prisoner. If they thought the female witnesses had been mistaken then they must acquit him. But if they believed them, was he sane at the time? In considering the prisoner's sanity they must set aside the issue of intoxication for he could not be acquitted on the grounds of drunkenness. On the other hand, there was much difference of opinion. Eminent medical men had been called as witnesses and it was reasonably clear that Dr Campbell had not always been himself. But at other times he had presented as perfectly sensible and sane. For example, he had made a fool of himself at Edinburgh in July but met the Asylum Committee four days later and conducted himself normally, concluding with an excellent speech of thanks. The day following the offence he made a rational statement to Dr Farquherson, saying he desired that a plea of insanity should be set up. He had thought of suicide but gave up that idea because he didn't want to deprive his wife and daughter of benefits under his insurance policies.

The judge strove to remain impartial. He turned to the evidence of Dr Hair and Dr Ogilvy-Ramsay. Was the prisoner's excitement as great as the two doctors said it was and such as to make him incapable and irresponsible he queried? And if he was insane, was this brought about by drink? It seemed clear that his condition was getting worse and that if he continued he would become hopelessly insane, probably from alcoholic poisoning. But had he reached that stage on 20 August? According to a number of eminent professionals he had shown signs of madness months, even years before, yet he was allowed to remain in post; the Visiting Committee met him monthly and saw nothing. Medical staff noticed his drunkenness but nothing else. He was allowed to remain Superintendent and might still have been in charge if he had not decided to resign.

Finally approaching the end of his summing up, the judge noted that in July last, the accused had actually given evidence that Michael Carr, a man on trial for murder, was insane, while he himself was apparently insane! However, one of the witnesses, Dr Yellowlees, believed he had lucid intervals between his attacks. If that was correct, was he insane or lucid on 11 August? The jury must consider first of all whether the prisoner did this act and if they found he did, whether or not he was insane at the time. They must hold the balance fairly but the prisoner must have been very mad indeed if he did the act and forgot that it was wrong.

It seemed that His Lordship had mixed feelings. The jury did not. They returned within twenty minutes with a verdict, finding the accused guilty, but insane at the time he committed the act and consequently not responsible for his actions at the time. Thereupon it was ordered that Dr Campbell be detained during Her Majesty's Pleasure and he was removed from the dock displaying no emotion.

No more was heard of him though we can probably assume that he was placed in some private institution and may even have been released back into the community eventually. Yet all these years later, with Garlands now demolished like similar institutions of its kind and so much advancement in psychiatric medicine, a question mark still hangs over the Campbell episode.

That the doctor's mind was becoming unhinged there seems little doubt but how ill was he at the time of the offence? We still don't really know, any more than those at the time really knew, some even denying he was insane at all, for clearly he did have lucid periods. He may have been drunk when he erred and genuinely couldn't recall the event or he may have undergone a psychotic episode and simply blotted out the unpleasant facts afterwards, which does appear more likely. Thus the verdict probably was the right one, but who can really say?

Whatever the true facts of the matter were, it was still a tragic end to what had once been an impressive career.

Chapter 31

Not Such an Inconspicuous Place
1888

She has been killing me by inches and driven me distracted and ruined my business ...

Ostensibly, it would seem there could be no more inconspicuous place to live than Carlisle's inner suburb of Denton Holme. A district of ordered terrace streets, it came into being in the 1850s, mainly to accommodate those working in nearby factories. The factories have now almost all gone or have changed their function but the houses remain, continuing to give off an air of quiet respectability. Despite an increase in motor vehicles and its regrettable loss of manufacturing industry, Denton Holme is still a safe cultural backwater, inhabited by respectable ordinary folk.

Denton Holme in 2005. Andrew Richardson

Yet though most locals are now probably unaware of the fact, Denton Holme has featured in its time a man who, driven to despair, butchered his wife and then himself in a macabre early morning ritual, and a woman fortunate to escape trial for treason. Both resided in houses in very close proximity to one another. They were Richard Glaister, and Margaret Cairns White.

Glaister's house in Westmorland Street is still there, uncannily almost unaltered; the same could be said for the house in Nelson Street where White lived. It is doubtful if White ever realized she was doing any great wrong. Glaister on the other hand was fully aware of what he was about and even wrote to the local press, apprising them of his intentions beforehand.

His appeared to be the case of a mind at the end of its tether, though at one time he had been as personable as White and there weren't many years dividing them. But there the similarity ended. Whereas she left Denton Holme in search of what she saw as new challenges, he came to live there when all else had irrevocably failed for him.

It hadn't always been like that for Richard Glaister. At the onset the future appeared bright. He and his wife Jane were natives of Abbeytown and, following their marriage, had stayed there after their first child was born. They lived in comfortable circumstances and had few if any financial worries. Richard earned good money as a commercial traveller with the firm of Copestake, Moore and Co., a London firm of drapers, and the family's future appeared assured.

All this changed in the mid 1880s when he was involved in a road accident and sustained serious head injuries. He recovered after a fashion but those in and around Abbeytown began to notice that his behaviour had become different. In short, he had lost his former ambition and enthusiasm for work and had become decidedly odd. As time passed and he made no attempt to seek new employment, money became scarcer and it was his father-in-law who was eventually providing most of the financial support.

Finally, in 1886, with his father-in-law's backing, the troubled thirty-six year old man went into the drapery business at Scotby. But this venture failed after only fifteen months and he and his wife and offspring came to live in the small terraced house in Westmorland Street where the tragedy would occur, now with an additional mouth to feed.

As was later to be revealed, Glaister felt his wife had let him down at Scotby, but only really wanted peace of mind. Given that his wife was again pregnant and that they were once more dependent upon her father, this scarcely appeared a likely option. Clearly an emotional woman as well as one who had been accustomed to better standards, she nagged him constantly. He responded with threats of physical violence though stopped short of harming her. But tension continued to gather momentum within the small cramped house.

Today Richard Glaister and his family might have benefited from some kind of social work involvement. This and regular invalidity payments would have kept the situation more stable as well as allowing a breathing space; for the thirty-three year old wife was still prepared to try and save the marriage. As recently as November 1887 she had given birth to a third child, so there was still some bond between husband and wife, fragile though this had became. But unfortunately, there were no tangible outpatient services or welfare cash available in those days. Left to his own devices, the husband remained unmotivated, while being constantly reminded too, that his father-in-law was the financial mainstay.

Meanwhile, the small family were socially isolated in Westmorland Street to the extent that Jane Glaister had been forced to call upon a local shopkeeper's wife, a Mrs Dodd, to assist her when giving birth again the previous November. The Dodds were the nearest thing they had to friends in Denton Holme. Presumably Glaister's moods and his wife's temper had gradually driven others away, including family members.

Christmas 1887 came and went and Richard Glaister was no closer to affording his wife any grounds for optimism. Yet they continued to keep up appearances and as late as Friday, 20 January, strolled out together to have the new baby vaccinated, calling in to exchange a few words with the wife's brother, William Messenger, on their way home. The fact that Messenger had a thriving drapery business in Lowther Street probably did nothing for Glaister's continuing lack of self-esteem.

He had other reasons for despair. What only Mrs Dodd knew outside the immediate family was that his wife had finally decided to leave him the following morning. He had been told but had chosen to remain unresponsive. A carrier was due to remove a few personal items. The eldest child was already with its paternal grandparent at Silloth. Jane Glaister intended to join him there with the two younger children. The husband was to be left to fend for himself. Possibly the aggrieved woman felt the move might finally bring him to his senses and jolt him into seeking work.

What she didn't know was that Richard Glaister had already posted two letters to the *Cumberland News* late that same evening, before returning home slightly the worse for drink. The couple retired to sleep in their first floor bedroom facing onto the street, after settling the two children down. Soon silence reigned.

Around 7.45 the following morning the Glaisters' neighbour, John Bell, heard a sudden cry from behind the bedroom wall: 'Murder! I'm done, I'm done, I'm done!' Gurgling noises followed. Bell didn't know what to do. Probably he had heard rows before and was aware that Glaister was an odd man. He, no doubt, had misgivings too, like many another, of getting involved in a domestic dispute. He decided that the failed draper may have been trying to strangle his wife, but rationalized non-involvement by telling himself that Jane Glaister must have come round. He went off to his work. Though he later came in for criticism, it is fair to say that had he raised the alarm, it would have been too late anyway.

Mrs Dodd on the other hand didn't feel she had the luxury of opting out. She had been requested by her friend to give her a knock at 8 o'clock that morning but felt uneasy, realizing how unstable the husband was. After knocking repeatedly and receiving no reply, she went to William Messenger's shop in Lowther Street. A local joiner was called in and finally gained entry to the house around 11 am.

A terrible sight met his eyes. Jane Glaister was lying with an arm and a leg hanging over the disordered blood-soaked bed. She was only partially dressed and lying on her face. When turned over it was revealed that she had deep cuts across her left cheek and throat and was quite dead. Her hands too were cut; evidently she had fought back at the onset but to no avail. The two year old child was playing with its mother's dangling foot, affording a further macabre touch to the scene.

Richard Glaister was in an even worse state. He was huddled up in a bloody heap at the top of the bed. His throat was cut so violently that the windpipe and gullet were completely severed. Still clutching a bread knife, he had almost beheaded himself. Paradoxically, the baby was lying unharmed at his feet.

Shortly afterwards a larger unused knife was discovered under the mattress. It was obvious that Glaister had meant business. This was confirmed by the two pieces of correspondence, which were published a few days later in the local newspaper. The first was dated Tuesday, 17 January. It must have been held over. Perhaps the tormented man had hoped even then that the situation might be resolved, though obviously it was not to be. His wife had became determined to depart with the children and he was equally determined that she should not, hence the final bloody deed.

Both letters are reproduced here, giving a clear picture from the broken man's perspective. Both were addressed to the editor:

Sir Kindly ask Mr Messenger of Cow Lane, Silloth and Mrs Glaister of Lesson Hall, Wigton, to see the letters. Then you will get full particulars of our end. It's been her cursed temper and her tongue that has caused this affair, to say nothing of the use of her hands. She has been killing me by inches and driven me distracted and ruined my business; but it's all over now, and may God have mercy upon our souls, protect our dear children, and keep them from harm.

May this be a lesson to all to live happily together; forgiving and forgetting, not to be continually upcasting everything and instead of making houses happy, trying to make them miserable. Many in Scotby can tell what my fate was, and how, at the last she acted as she said knavishly with Dobinson and Son against my wishes, and even got a solicitor to assist her to do it, whilst I for peace had to hold my tongue. Send a copy of your paper to Copestake and Co., of London.

Yours truly 'R Glaister'

The second letter was more concise but similar:

Westmorland Street, Friday Night.

Dear Sir I've lived as long as I could and no longer than I could for peace in this world. I now fly to the next to get peace and rest for my poor shattered head and mind. Had I only had peace and kindness at home all would have been well; but only to get worried and cursed and sworn at, battered and all kinds of threats is more than I can bear. May God have mercy upon my soul; I may part with my loving children, but death will only do it. God knows it and into his all merciful hands do I commend my soul and hope and trust that my father-in-law and my mother will see that they are not abused now that Janie and I are gone.

Believe me, yours truly 'R Glaister'

The verdict at the inquest was that J E Glaister was wilfully murdered by Richard Glaister and that Richard Glaister committed suicide while in a temporary fit of insanity. Both he and his wife were buried a few yards apart at Abbeytown and the children placed with their grandparents. This had to be one of the most tragic crimes in Carlisle, ensuring that Denton Holme was no longer such an inconspicuous place after all. But the area would achieve further notoriety following the conduct of Margaret Cairns White, the subject of our final study.

Chapter 32

Denton Holme's Tokyo Rose 1939–45

His wife had been deemed almost as treasonous in some quarters.

argaret Cairns White does not fall within the general time frame of this work, nor did she offend in Cumberland. Nonetheless, she is worthy of a place here, anyone else of her kind in the county having been virtually non-existent and the seeds of her later treasonous activities having had their origins in and around Carlisle.

She was an only child, born in Manchester in 1911 but brought soon to Carlisle where she lived for almost a quarter of a century in Nelson Street with her parents, her father being a manager with Morton Sundour Fabrics. A bright child, she was educated at Carlisle High School for Girls and regularly attended Church of England services. Hopes of a stage career having come to nothing, she opted for something more conventional, taking a commercial course and becoming a secretary with her father's firm on nearby Denton Hill, where she progressed well.

No one could have faulted the young woman until now. She was the product of an ordinary but respectable church-going family, had progressed well at school, been ambitious to the extent of training enthusiastically as a dancer and when this failed to provide her with a career, had changed course and become a successful white collar worker. Neither had she been short of suitors of the establishment type, including a doctor. She was not only intelligent and personable, but also attractive, above medium height, slim, with auburn hair and green eyes. Yet she was to sink to participating in activities which merited the close attention of MI5, spent months in solitary confinement and was debarred from the UK for many years. What caused her to go wrong?

We have to see the offending of Margaret White against the background of the period and environment in which she grew up. Her formative years were spent in a small provincial city following a disastrous war, which left whole countries in economic chaos. Carlisle was not immune, plunged back into the poverty and unemployment it had hoped was a thing of the past. Margaret White was cushioned against much of this by a father who continued in regular work, and by having eventually succeeded in consolidating her own position. But she was a thinking person and aware of the hardship all about her. This state of affairs grew no better as the 1930s advanced. It appeared ludicrous that England, still one of the richest countries in the world, should be subjected to hunger marches and means tests. She felt compelled to join one of the new radical parties attempting to bring about political change in Britain and elsewhere.

Given her upbringing and background, there could be no question of her joining the Communist party. But there was another political doctrine gaining ground and that was fascism, which, at that time, appeared to promise a great deal more to someone like her, with its emphasis on national pride and authority as well as an end to the dole queues. There was a charismatic English leader at its head too, Sir Oswald Mosley. Margaret White became one of his pioneer followers, convinced that she could assist in bringing his thinking to fruition locally.

In her spare time she began distributing Fascist literature in the city streets. In the black shirt and skirt of the female section of the movement, she spoke at Carlisle Cross. She participated in dancing displays at Fascist events and within a short space of time, was a key figure in the running of the Carlisle Women's Section. It has to be remembered that in the mid-1930s, Hitler still posed no tangible threat in the minds of the majority and Mussolini was seen as nothing short of a political messiah, both in Europe and America. Many people in Britain were interested in Mosley's fledgling Fascist movement, including members of the British aristocracy. By 1935 membership had topped 50,000 and its leader was confident he was a mere heartbeat from power. In Carlisle, the local press became sufficiently interested to send a reporter to Fascist HQ in Lonsdale Street. It was Margaret White who assisted in providing the visitor with favourable background information, duly published in the *Carlisle Journal*.

The main opposition came from the Communists. The manager's daughter made no secret of her loathing for them. When heckled at Carlisle Cross she gave back as good as she got though never became an outstanding speaker. That was left to Mosley and his immediate followers; they toured a wide area, espousing the merits of the new doctrine. Mosley was in Carlisle and its surrounding region several times between 1934 and 1936 and his Director of Propaganda,

Margaret Cairns White, bottom row, second from right, at Fascist Headquarters, Carlisle, in 1935. Cumbrian Newspapers Ltd.

William Joyce, spoke at the Queen's Hall in May 1935 to a large attentive audience with young men and women in black shirts in attendance as stewards.

It was all very exciting for a provincial girl. In fact Margaret already knew Joyce and as recently as February 1935, had organized a coach from Carlisle to Dumfries for those locals especially keen to hear him speak. The stocky, scar faced Irishman was a superb orator, invariably giving the impression of believing what he was preaching about. The restless girl from Denton Holme found him much more interesting than many of those she encountered. Joyce already had a wife but his marriage was in difficulties. No sooner was he divorced than she became his second partner in matrimony and they set up house in London.

By this time the British Union of Fascists was losing much of its earlier appeal in Carlisle and elsewhere though indeed, it is doubtful if most Cumbrians were ever fully convinced. The growing excesses of Hitler and Mussolini eroded any remaining enthusiasm. Joyce and his leader too had become increasingly alienated and finally parted company. For a time, Joyce became a language tutor, a task at which he excelled, but lost work when he refused to take Jewish students. His wife deplored this and there was never any evidence that she was ever anti-Semitic, or racist. However, there remained many tenets of fascism of which she didn't disapprove and within days of war breaking out in 1939, had accompanied her husband to Germany.

At the onset, there was no guarantee that the Nazis would accept them and they contemplated returning to Britain. But this didn't prove possible and internment would have been highly likely had they succeeded in doing so. In any case, with his keen intelligence and flair for languages, William Joyce quickly became a part of the Third Reich establishment, broadcasting daily to Britain in a propaganda capacity and continuing to do so until the end of the war, becoming better known as Lord Haw Haw.

His wife remained a shadowy figure. There were those who actually thought she had returned to Carlisle. In fact she had been offered a radio slot shortly after her husband began broadcasting and accepted it. Her remit was generally to chattily boost the good life of the German woman, as opposed to that of her British counterpart. In the beginning, like her husband, she was anonymous, but even when her name was later revealed, she never attracted the notoriety he did, albeit continuing at the microphone and taking a generous payment until 1945, when they were captured near the Danish border.

She had begun to lead at times, a dissolute life in Berlin, in which men and alcohol predominated. Even so, she may still have hoped that she and Joyce might be spared to lead a quieter life. Alas, he had incurred the resentment of too many people. Despite the fact that he had been born in America, grounds were still found to ensure that he was hanged for treason in January 1946 at Wandsworth Prison.

His wife had been deemed almost as treasonous in some quarters. Her career had been under scrutiny for several years by MI5 prior to the end of the war. She may have never commanded the audiences her husband did but had accepted payment from the enemy for her broadcasting activities, had been awarded the Nazi Civil Merit Medal, as well as taking German citizenship. If some writers like Boveri and West were prepared to consider her of little, if any, significance, the British establishment were not. It has even been suggested that her husband did a clandestine deal with the authorities on her behalf. It is certainly significant that she was never charged with treason, but was not allowed to walk free immediately either.

Returning to Germany following her husband's execution, she languished in internment there for two years and it was 1955 before she was finally allowed to live in Britain again. By this time most of her links with Carlisle had gone and it is doubtful if she would have been welcome back there in any case. She spent the remainder of her life in London where she died an alcoholic in 1972. She was still only sixty-one years old.

There were fewer women than men who broadcast for the enemy during the Second World War. Most of those who did tended to be insignificant figures but not all of them. Our final subject runs perhaps a close second to Iva Toguri, better known as Tokyo Rose, the American national who broadcast to US troops from Japan. Both were intelligent and not inherently evil but a prey to history and political circumstances, allowing themselves to be used to their lasting detriment; one ultimately spending ten years in prison, the other being spared, but dying in loneliness and ignominy, her time and talent squandered. It was all a far cry from Denton Holme.

Bibliography

Material from the following publications may be of additional interest to readers who wish to research further.

Amos, William, *Tales of Old Cumbria*, Countryside Books, 1996

Ashbridge, Ian, *Cumbrian Crime from a Social Perspective 1834–1894*, Redburn, 1999

Bragg, Melvyn, *The Maid of Buttermere*, Hodder & Stoughton, 1978

Brown, James Walter, *Round Carlisle Cross* (Omnibus edition) Thurnam, 1951

Dent, William, *The Cotton Barons' Church*, Colophon Press, 1991

Evans, Arthur, *Lake County Villains*, Red Earth Publications, 1993

Farish, William, *The Struggles of a Hand Loom Weaver*, privately printed, 1889

Farndale, Nigel, *Haw-Haw – The Tragedy of William and Margaret Joyce*, Macmillan, 2005

Ferguson, Richard S., *History of Cumberland*, Elliot Stock, 1890

— *The Royal Charters of the City of Carlisle*, Thurnam, 1894

MacDonald Fraser, George, *The Steel Bonnets*, Barrie and Jenkins, 1971

Mounsey, George G., *The Occupation of Carlisle in 1745*, Steel, 1846

Nelson H.P., *Doctor Harry The Story of a Country Doctor in Brampton*, compiled and edited by Tony and Mary Hopkins, printed by Wards of Gateshead

Scull, Andrew T., *Museums of Madness – The Social Organisation of Insanity in Nineteenth Century England*, Allen Lane, 1979

Smith, Kenneth, *Carlisle*, Dalesman Books, 1984

Topping G. & Potter J.J., *Memories of Old Carlisle*, Steel Bros, 1922

Towill, Sidney, *Georgian and Victorian Carlisle Life, Society and Industry*, Carnegie Publishing Ltd., 1996

Tullie, Issac, *Siege of Carlisle*, Samuel Jefferson, 1840

Index